Marketing Research:
A Computer-Assisted Approach

D.A. Schellinck
R.N. Maddox

Associate Professors of Marketing
Dalhousie School of Business Administration

THE DRYDEN PRESS
New York   Chicago   San Francisco
Philadelphia   Montreal   Toronto
Hong Kong   London   Sydney   Tokyo

Acquisitions Editor: Rob Zwettler
Project Editor: Jan Doty
Design Director: Alan Wendt
Production Supervisor: Diane Tenzi
Director of Editing, Design, and Production: Jane Perkins
Copy Editor: Siobhan Granner

Library of Congress Cataloging-in-Publication Data

Schellinck, Douglas Anton, 1949- Marketing research.
1. Marketing research–Data processing. 2. Marketing
research–Statistical methods–Data processing.
I. Maddox, R. Neil (Raymond Neil), 1938-
II. Title.
HF5415.2.S32 1987 658.8'3'0285 86-29029
ISBN 0-03-010924-8

Printed in the United States of America
789-090-987654321

Address orders:
383 Madison Avenue
New York, NY 10017

Address editorial correspondence:
One Salt Creek Lane
Hinsdale, IL 60521

THE DRYDEN PRESS
HOLT, RINEHART AND WINSTON
SAUNDERS COLLEGE PUBLISHING

Cover Source: Produced by Romulus Productions, Inc., New York, NY;
Director—Dr. Peter Crown; Programmer—Stan Cohen; Copyright 1981 MSDI.

Lotus 1-2-3 is a registered trademark of Lotus Development Corporation.

The Dryden Press Series in Marketing

Balsley and Birsner
Selling: Marketing Personified

Barry
Marketing: An Integrated Approach

Blackwell, Engel, and Talarzyk
Contemporary Cases in Consumer Behavior, Revised Edition

Blackwell, Johnston, and Talarzyk
Cases in Marketing Management and Strategy

Block and Roering
Essentials of Consumer Behavior, Second Edition

Boone and Kurtz
Contemporary Marketing, Fifth Edition

Churchill
Marketing Research: Methodological Foundations, Fourth Edition

Dunn and Barban
Advertising: Its Role in Modern Marketing, Sixth Edition

Engel, Blackwell, and Miniard
Consumer Behavior, Fifth Edition

Futrell
Contemporary Cases in Sales Management

Futrell
Sales Management: Behavior, Practice and Cases

Green
Analyzing Multivariate Data

Hutt and Speh
Industrial Marketing Management: A Strategic View of Business Markets, Second Edition

Kurtz and Boone
Marketing, Third Edition

Marquardt, Makens, and Roe
Retail Management: Satisfaction of Consumer Needs,
Third Edition

Park and Zaltman
Marketing Management

Rachman
Marketing Today

Rosenbloom
Marketing Channels: A Management View, Third Edition

Schary
Logistic Decisions: Text and Cases

Schellinck and Maddox
Marketing Research: A Computer-Assisted Approach

Schnaars
MICROSIM
A marketing simulation available for IBM PC ® and Apple ®

Sciglimpaglia
Applied Marketing Research

Sellars
**Role Playing the Principles of Selling: College and University
Edition**

Shimp and DeLozier
Promotion Management and Marketing Communications

Talarzyk
Cases and Exercises in Marketing

Terpstra
International Marketing, Fourth Edition

Young and Mondy
Personal Selling: Function, Theory, and Practice, Second Edition

Zikmund, Lundstrom and Sciglimpaglia
Cases in Marketing Research

Zikmund
Exploring Marketing Research, Second Edition

FOREWORD

What have we here? What we have is an innovative approach to helping students master the material covered in the marketing research course by harnessing the power of the microcomputer. This approach has a number of major advantages. First, complex concepts are demonstrated, not just described. For example, the user actually experiences what happens when one repeatedly draws samples of varying sizes from a population. This is an experience one is unlikely to have in a lifetime as a marketing research professional.

Second, the speed and computational power of the computer are brought to bear to assist in the learning process. It used to be said that marketing Ph.D.s did one multiple regression for their dissertation and that if they learned nothing else from the thesis, they learned that they never wanted to do another multiple regression. We feel that the same situation prevails in the marketing research course today, and that a package of this sort can help to bridge the gap between what is taught and what is used.

Finally, The micro is much more "user friendly" than mainframe computers. These programs are completely menu directed. It is not necessary to spend a major period of time learning to run the computer, or the programs, in order to realize the benefits. If you can play a video game, you can use these exercises.

We have included a large number of exercises to meet a wide variety of needs and course structures. Most instructors probably will not assign all of them. (Neither of the authors uses all of the exercises in the research course, and they do not use the same subset.) Give those that are not assigned a try. Many are simply fun and provide an opportunity to learn something painlessly above and beyond the stated content of the course painlessly.

The case data files are stored in a simple ASCII format. If you wish to analyze them with another statistical package, this is a simple matter. Any word processor can be used to make the changes necessary for input into the routine you want to employ. In most cases, all that is required is to delete the lines with variable names and change the semicolons separating the values to commas.

Package

An *Instructor's Manual* is available free upon adoption of this text. It contains case discussions, teaching notes, and solutions to problems in the book. **Most importantly**, it contains the two floppy disks to be used in conjuncton with the text. The disks are fully copiable and available for the

IBM PC and compatible computers.

Finally, while it is important to note that this supplemental text can be used successfully with any available marketing research textbook, we have also included a special matrix in the *Instructor's Manual*. This matrix keys suggested cases and exercises in this text to the appropriate sections found in two Dryden Press marketing research textbooks: *Marketing Research: Methodological Foundations,* Fourth Edition, by Gilbert Churchill (1987), and *Exploring Marketing Research,* Second Edition by William Zikmund (1986).

ACKNOWLEDGMENTS

We are indebted to more people than we can ever begin to mention. Tom Carter of the Dalhousie Microcomputer Information Center was extremely helpful early in the project, particularly in the development of the Eastern Food Distributors case. Keith Clarke, our colleague in the Dalhousie School of Business Marketing Group, co-authored and helped program the Feelgood case. The programming assistance of Jeff Scrutton and Vincent Richman was invaluable. Credit for the attractive screens and easy-to-use menus goes entirely to Jeff. Tina Morton, as well as others in the Business School, worked diligently at the task of turning nearly unintelligible drafts into a readable manuscript. Tim Roberts's skills at programming, particularly using LATEX, were essential for converting typewritten manuscript into final text.

We could not have completed the project without the expertise and willing assistance of those associated with the Dalhousie School of Business Courseware Development Project. This project is funded in part by the Bank of Nova Scotia and Digital Equipment Corporation. We also express sincere appreciation for the many valuable suggestions from the reviewers, Professors Paul Bloom, Tom A. Buckles, Lowell Crowe, Michael Hymen, Dennis McConnell, and blind reviewers whose identity is unknown to us.

Finally, a sincere thanks to our wives and children who bore the real brunt of this task. They were left to fend for themselves while we happily played with our (microcomputer) toys long into the night.

To the Student

The text *Marketing Research: A Computer-Assisted Approach* is accompanied by two microcomputer disks. Please request from your instructor information on how to obtain the disks.

D. A. Schellinck
R. N. Maddox

Halifax, Nova Scotia
January 1987

Contents

FOREWORD   v

1 INTRODUCTION   1
  1.1 Introduction   2
  1.2 Using the Computer   3
      1.2.1 Equipment Needed   3
      1.2.2 Getting Started   4
      1.2.3 Data Disks   5
      1.2.4 Miscellaneous   5
      1.2.5 Ending a Session   6

2 THE DECISION TO DO RESEARCH   7
  2.1 City Telephone Ltd. (A)   8
      2.1.1 Company Background   8
      2.1.2 Product Management   9
      2.1.3 Market Survey 10
      2.1.4 Case Assignment 11
  2.2 City Telephone Ltd. (B) 12
      2.2.1 States of Nature 12
      2.2.2 Probabilities of Each State 14
      2.2.3 Possible Research Results 15
      2.2.4 Action Options 17
      2.2.5 Possible Decision Payoffs 18
      2.2.6 Case Assignment 23
  2.3 How to Use the Bayesian Analysis Program 25

3 THE MARKETING INFORMATION SYSTEM   33
  3.1 Feelgood Headache Remedy (A) 34
      3.1.1 The Model 37

	3.1.2	The Submodels	38
	3.1.3	Marketing Mix Impact Model	48
3.2		Feelgood Headache Remedy (B)	51
3.3		Changing the Model	53
	3.3.1	Getting into the Model	53
	3.3.2	Some Hints	54

4 THE BASICS OF SAMPLING   **55**

4.1		The Accuracy of Mean Estimates	56
	4.1.1	Speedway Bus Lines	56
	4.1.2	Estimating Frequency Distributions	59
	4.1.3	Distribution of Mean Estimates	60
	4.1.4	Sampling Distribution of the Means	61
	4.1.5	Determining Accuracy	61
	4.1.6	Confidence Interval	62
4.2		Random Sample Number Generator	65
	4.2.1	Sampling from the Telephone Book	66

5 DETERMINING SAMPLE SIZE   **69**

5.1		Sample Size Analysis	70
	5.1.1	Calculation of Sample Size in Estimation Problems Involving Proportions	71
	5.1.2	Calculations of Sample Size in Estimation Problems Involving Means	74
	5.1.3	Determination of Sample Size in Problems Involving Hypothesis Testing of Proportions	75
	5.1.4	N (Population Size)	76
	5.1.5	Calculation of Sample Size for Hypothesis Testing Problems Involving Means	77
	5.1.6	Calculation of Sample Size When Testing Differences in Proportions Derived from Two Segments	77
	5.1.7	Calculation of Sample Size When Testing for Differences in Means Derived from Two Segments	79
	5.1.8	Assignment Questions	80
5.2		Stratified Sample Analysis	86
	5.2.1	Some Theory	86
	5.2.2	Program Input	87
	5.2.3	Program Output	91
	5.2.4	Assignment Question	94

6 APPLIED SAMPLING   **97**

  6.1   Eastern Food Distributors 98

      6.1.1   The Situation 98

      6.1.2   The Effect of Sampling Decisions on Survey Results . 103

      6.1.3   Case Assignment 111

  6.2   How to Run Eastern Food Distributors 114

      6.2.1   Selection of Incentives and Number of Mailings 114

      6.2.2   Selection of Respondent Selection Criteria 117

      6.2.3   Survey of Nonrespondents 118

      6.2.4   Visiting Business and Government Employees 118

      6.2.5   Survey of Tourists 118

7 QUESTIONNAIRE DESIGN   **119**

  7.1   OMNIBUS POLLS 120

      7.1.1   The Omnibus Poll 120

      7.1.2   Case Assignment 127

8 STAT   **131**

  8.1   Introduction to STAT 132

      8.1.1   Creating a Data Set 132

      8.1.2   Missing Values 134

      8.1.3   Subprograms 134

  8.2   Subprogram Instructions 137

      8.2.1   Data Modification 137

      8.2.2   Frequencies 141

      8.2.3   Crosstabs 143

  8.3   STAT: Sample Runs 144

      8.3.1   Example 1: Analyzing an Existing Data Set 144

      8.3.2   Example 2: Entering New Data 150

9 UNIVARIATE DATA ANALYSIS   **161**

  9.1   Eat Easy Foods (A) 162

      9.1.1   Nova Packers' Positioning 163

      9.1.2   A New Opportunity: Project Quick 'n Good 165

      9.1.3   Concept Tests 166

      9.1.4   Case Assignment 171

10 BIVARIATE AND MULTIVARIATE ANALYSIS   **175**

  10.1 Sail A' Way (A) 176

     10.1.1 Data 177

     10.1.2 Analysis 177

     10.1.3 Case Assignment 178

  10.2 Sail A' Way (B) 180

     10.2.1 Creating Sail A' Way 182

     10.2.2 Expansion Time 182

     10.2.3 Case Assignment 184

  10.3 Eat Easy Foods (B) 185

     10.3.1 Case Assignment 186

  10.4 Eat Easy Foods (C) 187

     10.4.1 Quick 'n Good Questionnaire 188

     10.4.2 First Results 190

     10.4.3 Case Assignment 192

  10.5 Trident Theater Company (A) 195

     10.5.1 Revenue Sources 196

     10.5.2 A Try at Fund Raising 199

     10.5.3 Case Assignment 201

  10.6 Trident Theater Company (B) 202

     10.6.1 Case Assignment 203

11 FORECASTING AND MARKETING TESTING   **211**

  11.1 Arctic Telephone Case 212

     11.1.1 Assignment 217

     11.1.2 Promotion Test Data 218

  11.2 Creating Tables and Graphs 221

     11.2.1 Creating a Table 221

     11.2.2 Creating a Graph 223

Chapter 1

INTRODUCTION

1.1   Introduction

"If God had meant us to use computers he would have put an RS232 port in our belly button!" That is the comment we receive from those who hate staring at the big green screen. Learning to find the right keys to push can be a monumental task. But, like it or not, the computer will increasingly be a part of the marketing manager's life support system. The marketing manager will be using the computer for data retrieval, simulations, analysis, and as a tutor to develop or refresh skills necessary for the job.

In developing the text and programs we have tried to immerse you in the micro-support environment you should encounter on the job. (If it is not there when you arrive, it is not expensive these days to create it.) The advantage of the microcomputer over minicomputers and mainframe systems is that software tends to be easier for the novice to use. So even if you can't find the right key you can keep on pushing until something happens.

There are three main types of programs on the disks and several user data sets. Three of the programs are simulations; Speedway Bus Lines, Eastern Food Distributors and Omnibus Polls. These programs/cases require you to make decisions about some element of study design (sample size, incentives, sampling frame and questionnaire design) and the simulation produces results of the survey which take into account your decisions. You can then go back and change your decisions in order to determine the possible impact on results.

Five of the programs are utilities; Bayesian Analysis, Random Sample Generator, Sample Size Analysis, Stratified Sample Impact Analysis, and STAT. Each of these utilities has a case, or set of questions, which help you learn how to do these types of analysis. The major value of utilities, both as a learning tool and a management tool, is that they allow you to perform sensitivity analysis. You can go back and determine the sensitivity of output to changes in input. Those of us who "dial tone" when they see an equation often learn more by playing with the program/equation than by studying the logic of the mathematics.

The third type of program is a spreadsheet template which will require you to use a spreadsheet package compatible with a *Lotus* file. The spreadsheet program is a powerful analytical tool that can be used by the market researcher for developing models to simulate the market environment (Feelgood Headache Remedy) and for data analysis and presentation (Arctic Telephone). Once the template is set up, the analysis is relatively easy and should illustrate to you the power of the program for these types of applications.

Most of the cases are drawn from real life situations. We have left in the many side issues, constraints and personality factors that impinge upon any management decision. This fits with our concept of the computer as a tool for facilitating the manager's decision process, not as a maker of decisions. Read the cases carefully as the situation usually must be taken into account when arriving at your answer.

To use these, and all the programs, without developing the urge to throw the computer through the wall, you should first read the material on how to use the program and be familiar with the theory which is described in your marketing research text. In many of the cases and questions you are not given enough information to arrive at a single solution. Use the power of the computer to conduct sensitivity analysis to determine the impact of various assumptions you will have to make.

Finally, do not throw this text and disks away when you have finished the course. You will likely find use for the utilities in other courses and it is worth holding on to a set of tools you will find useful on the job after graduation.

1.2 Using the Computer

Who should NOT read this section? You should not bother to read the following material if:

1. You designed the IBM PC.

2. You enjoy being the subject in instrumental conditioning exercises involving the computer's infinite capacity to deliver negative reinforcement (error messages).

3. Your basic approach to life is "When all else fails, read the instructions."

Otherwise, take a few minutes and read this section. A little time spent at the outset could prevent major amounts of grief later.

1.2.1 Equipment Needed

To run the programs on the accompanying disks you will need an IBM PC, or a "PC compatible," with two disk drives and a disk containing MS DOS.

Most programs can, in fact, be run on machines with a single disk drive, but it is less convenient. One program, Mean Estimation Tutorial, requires that the machine have an IBM Color Graphics card (or compatible) installed. If you try to run the program without a graphics card in the machine it will inform you that there is no graphics card and return you to the main menu. You will need to have a printer attached to take advantage of any of the options for producing printed output.

A word on compatibles. Compatibles, though excellent machines, are by definition a mixed lot. There are degrees of compatibility. The authors have run these programs on a wide assortment of machines without problems. However, it is always possible that some "compatible" may exist on which they will not run or on which some program will not work properly.

The instructions throughout this book have been written for the IBM PC. They will be appropriate for most machines on which these programs will run. Seek local assistance if an instruction does not seem appropriate for your computer.

1.2.2 Getting Started

For reasons lost in the Dark Ages starting up a computer is called booting, or booting up. To boot your computer you should place a disk with MS DOS, frequently referred to as a STARTUP disk, in the A drive. The A drive is usually the top drive or the left drive in a side-by-side arrangement. The DOS disk and all others should be inserted with the edge closest to the oval window first and the label up. A good way to remember is to place your right thumb on the disk label and do what comes naturally.

When the DOS disk is in place, close and latch the gate. Next turn the switches on your computer and the monitor to the on position. After a few seconds you will hear a whirring and grumbling and maybe sounds akin to a coffee grinder working on a handful of nails. The indicator light will go on indicating the computer is reading in data from the disk. When the drive stops and the light goes out you should see the DOS prompt **A>**.

At the prompt remove the disk containing MS DOS and insert disk 1 into drive A, close the door and type *MENU*. Then press the carriage return or enter key. This is the key on the right-hand side of the keyboard with the bent arrow pointing to the left ($\leftarrow$). After some more whirring and fussing you should see the main menu.

If the program you select does not work, check to see if your instructor has copied the file COMMAND.COM onto the disk. If not, you should copy this file from your MS DOS disk to both disks 1 and 2. You are now in business. Just follow the instructions. (Copywrite restrictions prohibit us from including COMMAND.COM on the disks as distributed.)

Handle all disks with care. Although they are amazingly durable, there are limits. Food and drink are the natural enemies of floppy disks. Never attempt to remove a disk when the light is on indicating that the drive is reading from the disk. Were you to do so you could damage the disk, the drive, or both.

The programs can also be copied onto a hard (fixed) disk and run from there. First go to drive C and make a directory (*MD name*). Then enter the directory (*CD name*). Put disk 1 into drive A and type *copy A:*.**. This should copy all the files from the disk to your directory onto the hard disk. Next copy disk 2. To run the program go to the directory and type *MR* followed by a return.

1.2.3 Data Disks

Some exercises permit you to save the results of your work as computer files. To do so you will need one and preferably two formatted disks. If you are unfamiliar with obtaining or formatting disks check with your instructor or lab supervisor, as appropriate. It would be a shame to spend time entering data for a couple of hundred cases and then not be able to save it for later use.

Any disk may be in any drive. To simplify things it is a good idea to establish a routine. Keep the program disk you are using in drive A and the disk to receive your data in drive B. If some other configuration is needed for an individual program, the instructions will tell you what is required.

If you will be using a hard disk to store your data files be sure to save them in the same directory you created for the programs.

1.2.4 Miscellaneous

We have termed these programs "user friendly." That is computer jargon and it is not quite true. A computer and its programs are benign, neither friendly nor unfriendly. These programs have been designed to be easy to use by anyone who is willing to be guided and follow a few simple prompts. The computer can do some things amazingly well. Thinking is not one of them. That must be left to the user.

Many programs allow you to make selections by moving the cursor using the arrow keys to the right of the typewriter keyboard. If a key is pressed

and the cursor does not move press the Num Lock key once and press the
arrow key again.

Typing errors can be corrected if they are caught prior to pressing the
enter or carriage return (C/R) key. Move the cursor back to the wrong
character using the backspace key($\leftarrow$). Type in the correct information. All
characters following the error must be retyped.

Be careful to enter the information you intend. The computer has absolute faith in you and will do whatever you tell it exactly, whether that is
what you meant or not. If you have entered data and told it to *END* rather
than *SAVE*, that's it; you have ENDED.

Be careful about mistaking the letters *O* and *l* for the numbers zero
(0) and one *(1)*. Do not separate numbers with commas, or input symbols
for units such as $, %, or #. Usually the computer will help you out if
you do. When it is expecting numeric input and you press another type of
character it will give you the error message *REDO FROM START*. This can
be irritating, but all you have to do is enter the correct quantity.

If things seem to be really fouled up simultaneously press the control and
c keys (Ctrl C) to return to the disk's main menu. Simultaneously pressing
control and break (Ctrl Break) will return you to the DOS prompt. From
there you can always type *MENU* to start over again.

1.2.5   Ending a Session

Ending a session is simple. Wait until the indicator light is out. Remove
your program and data disks. Then follow your institution's procedures for
leaving a workstation.

Chapter 2

THE DECISION TO DO RESEARCH

2.1 City Telephone Ltd. (A)

It was May 1986. Jim MacDonald, supervisor of marketing research for City Telephone, scratched his head in dismay. He had just discovered by accident that Wally Lawless, product manager for paging services, needed a market survey in a hurry. Jim wondered how this situation had arisen and what he could do to prevent these emergencies.

2.1.1 Company Background

City Telephone was a telephone company headquartered in a medium-sized city. As part of its telephone services it offered tone-only paging and two types of voice paging services. Their own voice service, introduced in 1983, was a machine intercept type — the message was recorded verbatim and transmitted to the pager automatically. In 1983 they had bought out the paging service unit of their major competitor, Airwaves Paging Service, which offered an operator intercept service. That is, an operator took the message which was transmitted a few minutes later by another operator.

The local utility board which set the rules for the telephone company's operations had specified that City Tel was not allowed to offer a telephone answering service. Airwaves therefore continued to own and operate their answering service. This meant that the same operators and supervisors who were formally City Tel's competitors now wore two hats. They worked for their own firm's *answering* service and for City Tel's *paging* service. Soon after City Tel purchased Airwaves a new competitor, Fast Page, started business. City Tel management had heard rumors that the former owner of Airwaves paging service had a 25 percent interest in Fast Page (despite a clause in the purchase agreement forbidding any such involvement for at least 5 years), but a check of the registry of joint stocks did not list him as a major officer.

Research on the pager market had been conducted by the marketing research department in 1983 just after City Tel had purchased Airwaves. This research had determined that 20 percent–30 percent of the Airwaves customers were anti-telephone company and would leave its service at the first opportunity. Another 30 percent–40 percent welcomed the new owner and some felt they would switch over to the automatic voice service rather than the operator intercept service. The report concluded that City Tel could expect to hold on to anywhere from 40 percent – 75 percent of the former Airwaves customers in the years following the acquisition.

2.1.2 Product Management

Wally had been product manager of paging services since 1983. Each year
in June he put together a marketing plan for the upcoming calendar year.
To insure that the plan was up-to-date he would put in a special request to
Jim's marketing research department for rental figures for the three paging
service lines for the past year. Exhibit 2.1 illustrates the number of pagers
rented for all three types of paging services since 1983.

Exhibit 2.1
City Telephone Ltd.
Number of Pagers Rented by
Pager Type

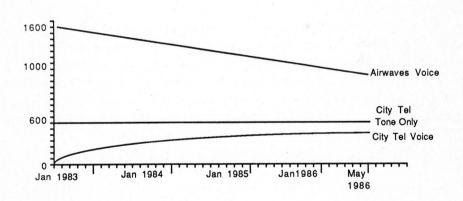

Sales of Airwaves voice service declined steadily from the initial 1,600
customers in 1983 to 1,000 customers by April 1986. This decline had been
offset by an increase in City Tel's voice service customers and it had been
assumed that they were simply switching services. However, when the May

1985 to April 1986 figures became available they showed that the growth in City Tel's voice pager rentals had stopped while Airwaves rentals continued to decline. Wally felt that perhaps he had been wrong in assuming that Airwaves customers had been switching to City Tel.

Other evidence also suggested that City Tel was losing customers to Fast Page. A recently created unit called the Competitive Intelligence Group had conducted a routine analysis of Fast Page earlier in 1986. The report had indicated that Fast Page was growing rapidly; faster, in fact, than City Tel's paging service.

2.1.3   Market Survey

Wally received the annual rental figures in mid-May, just four weeks before a two-day retreat where the nineteen product managers in the firm got together to discuss, defend, and coordinate their market plans. Remembering the reported growth of Fast Page, Wally felt there was a chance that the Airwaves service was losing customers to Fast Page. If true, this would call for a competitive response from City Tel in order to maintain market share. After consultation with his boss, it was decided that he should hire a student for the period of May 28 to June 15 to do a quick survey of those customers who had dropped the Airwaves paging service in the past year to determine why they were leaving.

Jim had overheard Wally asking a secretary to type a request to hire a student for research. Jim at first did not know how to respond. Eventually he approached Wally and asked if he could be of help. Wally explained what he intended to do and why. He had not gone to Jim because he felt Jim's staff was too busy to take on this "quick" survey. He intended to hire a student who would call the first 200 customers that had dropped the service and ask them why they dropped it.

Jim asked him if he had considered the potential difficulties in surveying these people? For example, reaching them could be difficult since most tended to be on the road. He also wondered if Wally had considered how to ask the question? He pointed out that simply asking them would not provide a reasonable answer. First, they are on the spot and many say something that doesn't offend, like "Your prices were too high." Second, there are usually many causal factors in any decision to drop a service and one question usually will not identify them. Since respondents say the first thing that comes to their mind the less obvious, but often more important, factors are missed. Wally saw the difficulties and said he would be happy if

Jim's staff could do the survey.

Jim came away from the meeting feeling that the episode was symptomatic of a larger problem. He felt the product managers in the company generally did not care whether the research was conducted properly and thus, relatively unsophisticated studies were viewed as sufficient basis for decisions. Alternatively, they viewed marketing research as a relatively simple task that anyone could do. Most had taken an executive development course that provided the basics of marketing research, so they felt confident enough to conduct basic research when the need arose.

Jim was glad to be doing the research, but Wally had been correct when he had said that Jim's staff was too busy to take it on. His budget had been set ten months previously, but he had several less important projects he could scuttle to obtain funds to do Wally's research. His real problem was that both his people were presently working overtime on other projects that had to be completed for the annual planning meeting. These projects were no less important.

He wondered how it had come to this. Was he at fault, was Wally, or was it an inherent problem in the way the company operated? And what could he recommend be done to improve things?

2.1.4 Case Assignment

1. What do you think might have caused the decline in Airwaves rentals? What are the possible marketing actions appropriate for each causal state?

2. What do you think might have caused the growth in City Tel's rentals? What are the possible marketing actions appropriate for each causal state?

3. What reasons might there be for the lack of research earlier by Wally?

4. Could Jim have done something earlier?

5. Is the budgeting system appropriate?

6. How effective is City Tel's Marketing Information System?

7. How can the marketing research process at City Tel, particularly the decision whether to conduct research, be improved?

2.2   City Telephone Ltd. (B)

Jim MacDonald, supervisor of marketing mesearch for City Telephone, needed a more rigorous means of deciding when to conduct research. A situation had arisen where he was being asked to conduct research that he felt might be a waste of time and money (see City Telephone Ltd. A).

He had received computer software several months earlier which had utilities designed specifically for marketing. One of the programs was a Bayesian Decision Analysis program which could be used to determine the value of proposed research. He decided to see if the program would be of use in this situation.

The first step was to gather the people who would have the information required. They were:

Wally Lawless. Wally was product manager for paging services. He had held this position ever since City Tel had purchased Airwaves Paging Services three years previously. Wally had been product manager for a wide range of telephone services over the past 15 years.

Don Gallant. Don had come to the company 13 years previously after receiving his masters in Engineering Physics and had been technical supervisor for paging services since joining. He was extremely knowledgeable about all technical aspects of providing paging services. He had observed, and frequently participated in marketing decisions over the years. His job required him to go into the field frequently to deal with customer problems.

Betty Verge. Betty was assistant supervisor of marketing research. She had been conducting research in the telephone industry for 6 years, and had joined City Tel a year and a half earlier. She had extensive training and experience in survey research.

Jim and the other three met for a scheduled four-hour meeting to decide on the appropriate information for input into the program. Jim began the meeting by demonstrating the program to Wally and Don. He then started through the program again, this time asking for input for the values requested.

2.2.1   States of Nature

They first had to decide how many states of nature there were. Jim explained that a state of nature generally referred to the customer response to a particular marketing strategy or tactic. In this case he suggested they define the states in terms of the causal factors that might have led to the downturn in City Tel's service, and the continued decline in Airwaves sales. It was important to identify the causal factors so that the effects of the actions they proposed to take could be predicted.

As a start it was suggested they brain-storm and come up with a list of causal factors. One suggestion was that the downturn was simply a statistical anomaly and that the situation would return to normal soon. However, this was rejected because the trend had continued for too long. In the end they came up with four possible causal factors.

1. A residual effect of the takeover. The decline in Airwaves rentals was a continued reaction to the purchase of Airwaves by City Tel. A survey conducted at the time had indicated that as many as 40 percent of the Airwaves customers (representing 640 pager rentals) might leave simply because they did not like the telephone company. The decline over the last three years of 600 rented pagers might be due mainly to the exodus of the anti-telephone segment. If this were true then the decline in rentals would be expected to stop soon without City Tel having to do anything more.

   If this was the reason for the decline in Airwaves rentals then City Tel must have been picking up new business over the last three years rather than customers switching from Airwaves to City Tel's service as had been thought. The most viable solution might be to stimulate primary demand.

2. Poor service at Airwaves. If, as was suspected, Airwaves management was not motivated to provide good quality service on behalf of City Tel (or as was also suspected, the owner had reason to want Airwaves customers to defect to Fast Page) then customers might have left because of the poor service offered by Airwaves. If this were true some might have switched to the City Tel service, but City Tel's reputation might also have been tarnished by association since both services were owned by City Tel. The customers might be turning to Fast Page instead.

   If this were true then it would be expected that the decline in Airwaves customers would continue with a substantial loss of customers in the next two years.

3. Fast Page's superior marketing strategy. Airwaves customers may have been switching to City Tel's service because of the attraction of an automated voice paging service, but Fast Page's marketing strategy

may have recently become more effective than City Tel's. This had happened previously with Airwaves before City Tel had purchased it. Airwaves as a competitor had been closer to its customers, had segmented the market effectively by offering special services and prices to real estate agents, doctors, people traveling throughout the market area, and so on. Its sales people had also proven to be more effective when going head to head with City Tel's sales people. As a result it established a strong reputation for being the best paging company and had taken away about 80 percent of City Tel's customers. It was possible that Fast Page was developing a similar reputation and that history was repeating itself.

If this were true then City Tel could expect to lose a large percentage of its customers unless considerably more effort were put into marketing the product and providing a good quality reliable service. Unfortunately due to regulatory constraints City Tel could not follow as detailed a segmented approach in its marketing strategy. The firm's strength was in the introduction of more automated services which allowed it to offer unique features.

4. Poor service at City Tel. The problem may have been customers' experiences with City Tel's automated voice paging service. As believed, customers may have been switching from the voice intercept service, but after a trial period they may have left. City Tel may have been picking up both new pager customers and those switching from the Airwaves service which caused the rental trend to continue to climb. However, as more people left the service word of mouth may have been creating a poor reputation for the service and fewer customers were starting the service or switching. Rather than go to another City Tel company they were going to Fast Page because it was the only other service in town.

   If this were true then City Tel would have to find some way of improving its automated voice service, or perhaps of preventing people from switching away from the Airwaves service.

2.2.2   Probabilities of Each State

Wally pointed out that all of these factors could have played a role in the decline, or lack of growth in City Tel's two services. Jim agreed that it was a shortcoming of the approach. He suggested that they also were restricted in the number of actions they could take, and that they would act as if at least one of these factors was the predominant cause of their troubles anyway. He asked Wally and Don to give their best estimates of the probabilities that each of these factors was the predominant cause of the situation. Wally felt the chances were that the problem lay mainly with the quality of service provided, although he could not decide whether the problem was more with City Tel or Airwaves. In the end he gave each of these states a .4 probability. His feeling was that the anti-telephone segment had long since defected and therefore only allocated a .05 probability to this state. That left a probability of .15 that Fast Page had a superior strategy.

Don said that he still frequently ran into the anti-telephone sentiment and felt that there was a .4 probability that that was the major cause of their problems. He, too, suspected Airwaves service might be poor and gave it a probability of .3. Having been involved with the pager service when Airwaves had stolen City Tel's market he felt there was a fair chance that history was repeating itself and gave the third state a .25 probability. He said he closely monitored the quality of the City Tel service and felt there was only a .05 probability that customers were leaving because of poor service.

2.2.3   Possible Research Results

Any research that was conducted would be expected to determine the cause of the decline in rentals. There were four possible results of the survey, one for each of the possible causes identified above. Don asked Betty to estimate the accuracy of research in determining which state actually existed in the market place.

Betty noted that the more money spent the more accurate the study was likely to be. To do a good job would cost roughly $10,000. To do a quick and dirty survey would only cost about $2,500, but the accuracy would be reduced. After some discussion Betty and Don came up with two sets of probabilities for the two grades of research (Exhibits 2.2 and 2.3).

Exhibit 2.2
Estimated Probabilities of
Research Results Given Each State
($10,000 study)

Actual Market States

Results of Research	1 Anti- Telephone	2 Poor Air- waves Service	3 Good Fast Page Service	4 Poor City Tel Service
State 1 Exists	.80	.05	.05	.05
State 2 Exists	.10	.80	.05	.05
State 3 Exists	.05	.10	.80	.10
State 4 Exists	.05	.05	.10	.80

Exhibit 2.3
Estimated Probabilities of
Research Results Given Each State
($2,500 study)

Actual Market States

Results of Research	1 Anti- Telephone	2 Poor Air- waves Service	3 Good Fast Page Service	4 Poor City Tel Service
State 1 Exists	.60	.10	.10	.10
State 2 Exists	.20	.60	.10	.10
State 3 Exists	.10	.10	.60	.20
State 4 Exists	.10	.20	.20	.60

2.2.4 Action Options

Next they had to decide what actions they might take to remedy the situation. They came up with a list of three actions.

1. Do nothing more than they are presently doing.

2. Improve the Airwaves paging service by moving the operation to City Tel's head offices and changing management. They would also advertise the improved service to attract those people who preferred an operator intercept paging service.

   This option would cost an estimated $300,000 over the next two years.

3. City Tel could focus on stimulating primary demand through increased advertising and salesforce support. This option would cost an estimated $100,000 over the next two years.

2.2.5   Possible Decision Payoffs

It ended up taking about three hours to decide what the possible impact of each action would be, given each state. They first estimated that approximately $720 in revenue was generated by each pager rented over the two-year period. They then decided on three sources of gains or losses in rentals (see Exhibit 2.4). The first source was primary demand, new customers who had to select from among the three services available. Second, Airwaves could lose or gain customers from the other two services. And third, City Tel could gain or lose customers from the other two services. If customers switched from Airwaves to City Tel then Airwaves would show a loss while City Tel would show a corresponding gain.

Exhibit 2.4
Projected Rental Gains and Losses
for the Do Nothing Action
(Two-Year Rental Equivalents)

States

Sources of Gain/Loss	1 Anti- Telephone	2 Poor Air- waves Service	3 Good Fast Page Service	4 Poor City Tel Service
Primary Demand	0	0	0	0
Airwaves	-50	-200	-200	-200
City Tel	0	0	-100	-100
Total Pagers Gained/Lost	-50	-200	-300	-300
Total Revenue Gained/Lost	-$36,000	-$144,000	-$216,000	-$216,000
Cost of Alternative	$0	$0	$0	$0
Payoff	-$36,000	-$144,000	-$216,000	-$216,000

The impact of the first action, do nothing, was easiest to calculate. If the decline was due to an anti-telephone segment defecting then this should stop soon. At most they would lose another 100 pager rentals over the next two years. Assuming half of them left in the first year, the impact would be the loss of the equivalent of 50 continuously rented pagers over the two years, or $36,000.

If there was a problem with Airwaves management then the decline would continue and they could expect to lose another 400 pager rentals, 200 two-year rentals, over the next two years. If the problem was a more effective Fast Page marketing strategy then they could expect to start losing customers from City Tel as well. The total impact would be a loss of 200 Airwaves and 100 City Tel two-year rentals. If the problem was poor City Tel service then they could expect the decline at Airwaves to continue and a decline at City Tel to start. Again the impact would be 200 Airwaves and 100 City Tel two-year rentals lost.

Improving the management and image of the Airwaves service would also cost $300,000 of which $250,000 would be allocated over the next two years ($120,000 in salaries and $130,000 in depreciation). This option was expected to reduce the percentage of customers switching away from the Airwaves service and to attract many of the new customers that might normally have gone to Fast Page. If the problem was poor management at Airwaves (state 2) then this action should generate about 300 new pager rentals over the two-year period (150 two-year rentals). Some of those leaving Airwaves were going to City Tel so this would mean a loss of 50 two-year rentals at City Tel for a net gain of 100 two-year rentals, a payoff of -$178,000 after the cost of the action was taken into account. (See Exhibit 2.5).

If the problem was an anti-telephone sentiment then they expected to lose about 50 two-year pager rentals for a total payoff of -$286,000. This action would be fairly effective if the problem was Fast Page's marketing strategy since the two services are similar. Airwaves would gain 100 two-year rentals, half at the expense of City Tel, for a payoff of -$214,000. If the problem was the poor automated voice service then the reduced switching would lead to fewer people leaving City Tel. The net loss would be 100 two-year rentals for a payoff of -$322,000.

Exhibit 2.5
Projected Rental Gains and Losses
for the Improve Airwaves Action
(Two-Year Rental Equivalents)

States

Sources of Gain/Loss	1 Anti- Telephone	2 Poor Air- waves Service	3 Good Fast Page Service	4 Poor City Tel Service
Primary Demand	0	150	100	0
Airwaves	-50	0	0	0
City Tel	0	-50	-50	-100
Total Pagers Gained/Lost	-50	100	50	-100
Total Revenue Gained/Lost	-$36,000	$72,000	$36,000	-$72,000
Cost of Alternative	-$250,000	-$250,000	-$250,000	-$250,000
Payoff	-$286,000	-$178,000	-$214,000	-$322,000

Another action being considered was to advertise the City Tel service more extensively and increase sales support to stimulate and attract potential paging customers. The total cost would be $100,000 over the next two years (see Exhibit 2.6). If the problem was an anti-telephone sentiment the loss of Airwaves rentals would be offset by the gain of rentals from primary demand for a payoff of -$28,000. This action would also offset the losses due to poor management at Airwaves for a payoff of -$100,000 if state 2 existed. The advertising campaign would have less effect on Fast Page's marketing strategy, giving a payoff of -$136,000. And finally, if there was a problem with City Tel's service, and word-of-mouth was negative then the advertising campaign would have little effect. They would expect to lose 300 two-year rentals for a payoff of -$316,000. The payoffs are summarized in Exhibit 2.7.

Exhibit 2.6
Projected Rental Gains and Losses
for the Increase Advertising and Sales Support
for City Tel's Service Action
(Two-Year Rental Equivalents)

States

Sources of Gain/Loss	1 Anti- Telephone	2 Poor Air- waves Service	3 Good Fast Page Service	4 Poor City Tel Service
Primary Demand	150	150	100	0
Airwaves	-50	-200	-200	-200
City Tel	0	50	50	-100
Total Pagers Gained/Lost	100	0	-50	-300
TotalRevenue Gained/Lost	$72,000	$0	-$36,000	-$216,000
Cost of Alternative	-$100,000	-$100,000	-$100,000	-$100,000
Payoff	-$28,000	-$100,000	-$136,000	-$316,000

Exhibit 2.7
Payoff Table
($000)

States

Possible Actions	1 Anti-Telephone	2 Poor Air-waves Service	3 Good Fast Page Service	4 Poor City Tel Service
Do Nothing	-36	-144	-216	-216
Improve Airwaves	-286	-178	-214	-322
Increase City Tel's Marketing Efforts	-28	-100	-136	-316

2.2.6   Case Assignment

1. Is there any action that should be ruled out right away? If the costs were allocated in a different way would your conclusion change? Could they have used different time frames when estimating the payoff of each action?

2. The problem could be any or all four of the hypothesized reasons identified by City Tel management. Are their simplifying assumptions appropriate?

3. In this case how sensitive is the derived value of information to:

   - Differences in opinion about the probability of each state?
   - The differences in the accuracy of the research?

4. How would you handle Wally and Don's disagreement over the state probabilities?

5. What is inherent in the market situation that leads to all the payoffs being negative?

6. Would you do the research? Would you do the $10,000 study or the $2,500 study?

7. Do you feel this type of analysis provides any benefits for the marketing manager or the marketing researcher?

2.3   How to Use the Bayesian Analysis Program

When you select Bayesian analysis you will first be asked to indicate the number of states of nature and of actions. (The numbers you would enter are shown in the small boxes on screen 1. The numbers used in the example are not drawn from the City Telephone case.)

Screen 1

```
                          Bayesian Analysis

          Number of States of Nature (2,3,4) :  2
          Number of Actions (2,3,4) :  2
          Number of Results (2,3,4) :  2




              Use ↑ ↓  to move around, PgDn for Next screen
```

The number of actions refers to the alternative actions, usually market strategy decisions, you are considering. For example, you may be considering whether to spend money on the salesforce, advertising, or an improvement on your brand. If you knew what the market response would be to each of these alternatives, you would have no problem deciding. If, however, you cannot judge the state of the environment, then you may require more information before you choose your action.

You will have to define the states of nature that exist. This is a fairly arbitrary decision since obviously an infinite number of states are possible. For guidance look at the actions you are considering and define your states in such a way that will give you a clear choice of action if a particular state exists. The fact that some states are less likely to exist is taken care of when you assign probabilities.

Sometimes you are faced with symptoms of a problem in the market place and there are several possible states of nature that might be causing it. In that case you would first decide on the states of nature and then define the actions appropriate to solve the problem.

In either case you will have to clearly define your states of nature and actions, before you start the program. The maximum number of states and actions is four.

Screen 2 requires you to specify what you feel the probability is that each state exists. Since these are assumed to be the only possible states of the environment, the sum of the probabilities must be 1. If you feel there is a 20 percent chance that state 1 exists type in *.2* and hit the return key. The computer will only let you enter values between 0 and 1. Also, you cannot go to the next screen until the probabilities add up to 1.

Screen 2

Bayesian Analysis
Probability Values of the Different States

S1: State 1 – Probability = $\boxed{.30000}$
S2: State 2 – Probability = $\boxed{.70000}$

SUM OF PROBABILITIES = 1.0000

Use ↑ ↓ to move around, PgDn for Next screen, and PgUp for Last screen

---

The Bayesian analysis does not allow for uncertainty in these estimates. In real world situations the person responsible for these estimations may have some uncertainty.

One way of handling the problem is to perform sensitivity analyses. The analysis is repeated with a low probability estimate (for example, the estimator feels there is only a 5 percent chance the true probability is below this value) and a high probability estimate. With three or more states you may have to try several combinations of high and low probabilities. If the answers are the same each time then there is no problem. If the answers differ then the decision maker will have to make a judgment call. Since the whole exercise is designed to help the decision maker, not to make the decision, this should not be a problem.

Screen 3 asks you to determine the payoff of each action given the existence of each state. The payoff is generally the expected profit of the action over the life of the investment. The units can be in dollars, thousands of dollars or millions of dollars. Generally speaking, an accuracy of four figures is sufficient. When talking about millions of dollars you would probably use thousands as your unit. The payoff can be negative for some (or all) of the states. The program will not accept decimal values.

Screen 3

Bayesian Analysis
Payoff Table Values for Decision Process

	S1: State 1	S2: State 2
A1: Action 1	400	-200
A2: Action 2	-100	300

The Expected Value of Action 1 - A1: Action 1 is -$20.00
The Expected Value of Action 2 - A2: Action 2 is $180.00

The Alternative with the Highest Expected Value is A2: Action 2.

Once you enter the values in the payoff table the computer will generate the expected value of each action and identify the alternative action with the highest expected value. You can obtain a hard copy of these results by hitting the print screen key. Make sure the printer is on first.

Screen 4 illustrates the arithmetic calculations that were used to derive the expected values so that you can see where they come from. This screen also shows the expected value under certainty and the expected value of perfect information, as well as the calculations used to derive these values. Examination of the calculations facilitates sensitivity analysis since it is easier to see how the input values affect the output values.

Screen 4

```
                      Bayesian Analysis
                   Expected Value Analyses


    The Expected Value of Action 1 A1: Action 1 is -20.00
 EV(A1) = (0.300)(400) + (0.700)(-200) = -20.00


    The Expected Value of Action 2 A2: Action 2 is 180.00
 EV(A2) = (0.300)(-100) + (0.700)(300) = 180.00




    The Expected Value Under Certainty is 330.00
 EV (Certainty) = (0.300)(400) + (0.700)(300) = 330.00


    The Expected Value of Perfect Information is 150.00
 EVPI = EV (Certainty) - EV (Optimum Action)
      = EV (Certainty) - EV (A 2)
      = 330.00 - 180.00 = 150.00




           PgDn for Next screen, and PgUp for Last screen
```

Often this is as far as you wish to go. If so, you can then either hit the ESC key to go back to the main menu, or the page up key to go back and change input values in order to perform sensitivity analyses.

Screen 5 measures the accuracy of the research you are considering conducting. You must input the probabilities of your research concluding each state exists, given the existence of each state. For example, if state 1 exists, you may feel that there is an 80 percent chance your research will conclude correctly that state 1 exists. You would therefore say there is a 20 percent chance the research will conclude, incorrectly, that state 2 exists. The accuracy of the results will generally increase with the cost of the research. However, sometimes the gain in accuracy is not worth the cost. If you have more than one research option, you should examine their impact on the value of research to help determine which research alternative is preferable.

Screen 5

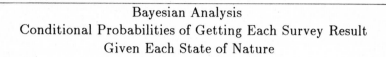

Bayesian Analysis
Conditional Probabilities of Getting Each Survey Result
Given Each State of Nature

	S1: State 1	S2: State 2
R1: Result 1	.8000	.3000
R2: Result 2	.2000	.7000
	1.000	1.000

Use ↑ ↓ to move around, PgDn for Next screen, and PgUp for Last screen

Screen 6 gives the posterior probabilities of each state existing given each research result. These values are then input into the calculations (illustrated on screen 7) of the expected value of each alternative, given each research result. Screen 8 shows the probability of obtaining each result. These three screens are shown to help you understand where the figures come from, and to facilitate sensitivity analysis. However, the values derived are in themselves not important and you can page down through them rapidly if you prefer.

Screen 6

Bayesian Analysis
Calculation of Posterior Probabilities

	Prior Prob P(S)	Cond Prob P(R/S)	Joint Prob P(RS)	Post Prob P(S/R)
R1: Result 1				
S1: State 1	0.300	0.800	0.240	0.533
S2: State 2	0.700	0.300	0.210	0.467
R2: Result 2				
S1: State 1	0.300	0.200	0.060	0.109
S2: State 2	0.700	0.700	0.490	0.891

PgDn for Next screen, and PgUp for Last screen

Screen 7

Bayesian Analysis
Expected Value of Each Alternative Given Each Research Outcome

R1: Result 1 Revised Probs: P(S1)=0.533 P(S2)=0.467
EV(A 1) = (400)(0.533) + (-200)(0.467)= 120.00
EV(A 2) = (-100)(0.533) + (300)(0.467)= 86.67
R2: Result 2 Revised Probs: P(S1)=0.109 P(S2)=0.891
EV(A 1) = (400)(0.109) + (-200)(0.891)= -134.55
EV(A 2) = (-100)(0.109) + (300)(0.891)= 256.36

PgDn for Next screen, and PgUp for Last screen

Screen 8

Bayesian Analysis
Probability of Obtaining Each Result

P (R1: Result 1) =
(0.300)(0.800)+ (0.700)(0.300) = 0.450
P (R2: Result 2) =
(0.300)(0.200)+ (0.700)(0.700) = 0.550

PgDn for Next screen, and PgUp for Last screen

The last screen (screen 9) shows the calculations of the expected value of research. This is derived by subtracting the expected value of the decision with research from the expected value of the decision without research. Again you might want to hit print screen in order to record these values.

Screen 9

Bayesian Analysis
Expected Value of Research

Expected Value of Research = EV (With Research) - EV (Without Research)
EV (With Research) = (0.450)(120.00)+ (0.550)(256.36)
= 195.00
EV (Without Research) = EV (A2: Action 2)
EV (Without Research) = (0.700)(-100.00)+ (0.700)(300.00)
= 180.00

Expected Value of Research = 195.00 - 180.00 = 15.00

ANALYSIS FINISHED: PgDn to run again, ESC to quit, or PgUp for Last screen

---

If you wish to exit the program at this point hit the Esc key. If you wish to start again then hit the PgDn key and the program will loop back to the first screen. If you do this the values you entered previously will be the default values.

Chapter 3

THE MARKETING INFORMATION SYSTEM

3.1   Feelgood Headache Remedy (A)

Maureen Barnett felt queasy. Having worked for OTC Drugs for only a few months as an assistant brand manager for the firm's laxative brand, Maureen thought she was really going places when she was offered the brand manager position for Feelgood headache remedy. She had snapped up the offer as a great promotion without any study of the brand. Now she wasn't so sure she had made the right move.

It turned out that sales had been declining at about 2 percent per year for the past ten years. Gary Norwood, one of OTC's market research supervisors, had answered Barnett's request for this information on the brand. Feelgood's market share had also been declining. In recent years it had lost about 1 percent of the market each year to the point that, as of 1986, it had an estimated 15 percent of the market.

As bad as this information was, this was not really what was bothering Barnett. Her major concern was the potential availability of funds to support her brand. Through the grapevine she had heard that upper management tended to categorize products using the Boston Consulting Group and Product Life Cycle approaches and to base all decisions on those categories. Feelgood was seen to be a dying product whose market position had placed it, in upper management's view, in the "Cash Cow" category. Upper management was reluctant to invest further in expenditures on advertising, promotion, or improvements to packaging or product form for "Cash Cows."

Feelgood still had a brand-loyal segment which allowed the company to charge a price above the purely competitive level and make a reasonable profit. The size of this segment was gradually decreasing and Barnett felt that this trend could be halted with proper marketing of the brand. The general thrust had been to reduce support and simply milk the product.

Barnett saw her mission as the maximization of profits from the brand over the long run. The simplest approach would be to maintain a high price. They would use some minimal amount of the contribution margin for advertising and promotion to remind the brand-loyal segment that the brand was still on the market and convince the trade to continue stocking Feelgood as had been the practice over the past five years. If the sales decline continued, she was afraid the brand would be cut, and in any event her future looked dim if she was perceived merely as a caretaker for a dying brand.

Barnett felt, however, that there was a good chance that investment in marketing, and a fine tuning of the marketing strategy, might substantially improve the outlook for both Feelgood and Maureen Barnett. She also had some fairly radical ideas which could possibly stimulate sales. However, without a stronger case for improved investment, upper management would not approve any market plan that required increased spending.

To build that stronger case, she realized she needed more information than she originally asked of Norwood. Unfortunately, there had been scant information collected on Feelgood by the market research department upon which to base any decisions. The last consumer research on the product had been conducted five years ago and it was probably unrepresentative of present attitudes and behaviors.

There was other, more current information, however, as OTC used a national survey company to monitor product movements. Therefore, they could estimate with a fair degree of accuracy the sales of its, and its competitors' brands. Reports could be broken down by dollars, units and package size. All commodity distribution shares were also potentially available for the headache remedy category, broken down by regions and outlet types.

Through Gary Norwood, Barnett knew that the market research department had been trying to obtain approval for the development of a more sophisticated marketing information system that could provide the detailed, up-to-date information OTC's brand managers needed. They, too, had been having a problem convincing upper management to invest. Upper management was unconvinced that the information could be usefully employed.

Barnett invited Norwood out for a power lunch to see if there might be some way to get the research department to help her build a case for increasing support for Feelgood. Over lunch she presented the proposition that helping her solve her decision support needs could help Norwood's desire for an improved general information system. As always, Norwood was happy to see a line officer interested in the value of research. He could see some long-term potential benefit in building a model sophisticated enough to be helpful in decision making, yet simple enough to be understood and trusted by Barnett.

Over coffee they began discussing the problem. Norwood recalled reading an article by John Little in the *Journal of Marketing* which had outlined the requirements for a Marketing Decision Support System (DSS). The article had pointed out that a DSS required more than data; it also required modeling, statistical and optimization capabilities. BRANDAID was one such marketing model mentioned in the article. Norwood suggested they examine the feasibility of modifying the BRANDAID model. He thought they should simplify it as much as was reasonable in light of their available data; and the qualities of the headache remedy market.

Norwood also knew that as beginners in the modeling business, a complicated model might overwhelm them and kill their hope for its future use with other managers. Barnett was very pleased with this suggestion, believing that such a model would be able to help in designing a market plan, and would make it more likely that upper management would approve the plan.

Immediately after lunch Norwood reread the Little article and started to work on a usable model for Feelgood. After some thought, and several conversations with Barnett concerning the important variables in her particular situation he wrote up a memo to Barnett outlining his view of a usable model. Exhibit 3.1 presents this memo.

Exhibit 3.1

To: Maureen Barnett, B.M. Feelgood
From: Gary Norwood, Supervisor, M.R.D.
Subject: Modified BRANDAID

After considerable thought, I think that the best way to present the model I am suggesting is to simply show the mathematical relations assumed in the model with some explanatory comments which are essentially my understanding of our conversations. After you have studied the model we should get together and decide if it meets your assumptions about the headache remedy market and whether it will assist you in your decision making. Here then is an overview of what I have put together.

Exhibit 3.1 continued

3.1.1 The Model

At first the notation to describe the model may be frustrating but it should turn out to be quite simple once you understand the jargon. The structure of the model is:

$$S(t) = S_o \prod_{i=1}^{I} e_i(t)$$

where:

$S(t)$ = sales of Feelgood in period t

S_o = Status Quo or reference brand sales rate

$e_i(t)$ = index of the effect on Feelgood sales of ith sales influence, $i = 1, ..., I$ (I = number of sales indices)

These effect indices (e_i) represent the impact of marketing mix and other important variables on sales. There could be a different effect index for each controllable variable, such as price, product, distribution, advertising, and promotion. Indices might also be developed for important uncontrollable variables such as growth trends, competitive activity, and seasonality.

At this point the important effects on sales appear to be:

1. Advertising

2. Salesforce activity

3. Pricing

4. Seasonality

5. Category sales trend

6. Promotions (such as case allowances and coupons)

To start building the model it was first necessary to set a reference level for sales, and for all the other indices. Based upon our conversations I have set the reference sales rate to our sales in the first quarter of last year: 5,000,000 equivalent units of Feelgood. Advertising was approximately $1,121,000 that quarter. You expressed the opinion that if the effectiveness

Exhibit 3.1 continued

of the media coverage and the message remained constant, you would expect sales to remain at about 5,000,000 units. I have used this budget figure in setting the advertising budget index. These standard levels of sales and advertising give effect indices of 1.0. All of the other indices were referenced in the same way. The equation now looks like:

$$S(t) = S_o \times e_1(t) \times e_2(t) \times e_3(t) \times ...e_i(t)$$
$$5,000,000 \text{ sales} = 5,000,000 \text{ reference sales} \times (1.0 \times 1.0 \times 1.0 \times ...1.0)$$

This equation has two important characteristics. First, a change in any index has a direct effect on sales. If you increase your advertising budget by \$20,000 to \$120,000 you might estimate this would increase sales by 10 percent. That is, the effect index would increase to 1.1, which would in turn increase the sales estimate by 10 percent.

$$5,500,000 = 5,000,000 \times 1.0 \times 1.1 \times .... \times 1.0$$

Second, the effects of all variables interact. Thus an improvement in the effect of advertising by 10 percent builds on an improvement in another variable such as salesforce activity (perhaps 20 percent) to give a combined effect of $(1.1) \times (1.2) = 1.32$ or a 32 percent increase in sales.

3.1.2   The Submodels

The model would not be of great value if every change in the effect indices was based on nothing more than "seat of the pants" estimates by you, or any other marketing manager. Instead submodels have been developed which take actual changes to the marketing mix and determine their potential impact on sales. The model I am suggesting we start with has five submodels. Each of these is described separately.

Advertising Submodel

The first value that must be determined is the rate which target market customers are exposed to persuasive advertising messages. This value is

Exhibit 3.1 continued

called the advertising rate $a_1(t)$ and is deemed to be a function of:

a. The amount spent on advertising Feelgood in period t, $X_1(t)$.

b. The media efficiency in period t, $h_1(t)$. This is based on the cost per thousand (CPM) of the media schedule, and is derived from the number of impressions delivered by the media vehicles used in the media schedule.

c. The effectiveness of the copy in influencing the customer $k_1(t)$. This is a judgmental index which measures the combined effectiveness of the creativity, attention-getting ability, communication ability, and the relevance of the messages during the period t.

I had to determine reference values for these three variables which would maintain sales at the reference level (h_{1o}, k_{1o}, X_{1o}). I used the \$1,121,000 advertising budget mentioned above for the advertising budget standard. You stated that our Advertising Plan called for a CPM of approximately \$3.40 so I used that as the reference for the media efficiency index. Since we are just starting the modeling process, and we haven't changed our creative approach drastically in the past several years, I arbitrarily set the copy index at 1.0.

The submodel is similar to the main model in that the three effects are standardized by dividing by the reference values so that they have a normal value of 1, and then multiplied by each other to come up with the unadjusted advertising rate, $A_1(t)$.

$$A_1(t) = \frac{h_1(t)}{h_{1o}} \times \frac{k_1(t)}{k_{1o}} \times \frac{X_1(t)}{X_{1o}}$$

In this case, with no changes, the equation is:

$$A_1(t) = \frac{\$3.40}{\$3.40} \times \frac{1.0}{1.0} \times \frac{\$1,121,000}{\$1,121,000} = 1.0$$

Exhibit 3.1 continued

An increase of 10 percent in the advertising budget would cause an increase of 10 percent in the advertising rate.

$$A_1(t) = \frac{\$3.40}{\$3.40} \times \frac{1.0}{1.0} \times \frac{\$1,233,100}{\$1,121,000} = 1.1$$

The advertising rate should be adjusted for the impact of advertising in following periods (memory effect). To do this the advertising rate in period t is thought of as a combination of the last period's advertising rate (say 30 percent) and this period's advertising rate (1 - last period's percentage, in this case 70 percent). The memory effect is based on the idea that people do not immediately forget the last period's advertising. By assuming some carry-over effect of advertising it becomes necessary to allocate the value of a period's ad budget over the periods in which it has some impact. This is analogous to viewing advertising as a capital investment and depreciating it over its useful life. The formula I suggest is:

$$a_1(t) = B_1 \times A_1(t-1) + (1 - B) \times A_1(t)$$

where:

$a_1(t)$ = memory-adjusted advertising rate for period t.

B_1 = memory effect (carry-over fraction of advertising).

But there is not a one-to-one ratio between advertising effectiveness and sales. You have told me that it is likely that you would be able to sell some Feelgood without any advertising at all. Similarly, after a point no amount of increased advertising would increase sales. The model must therefore determine $E_1(t)$, the basic effect on sales in period t of a particular memory-adjusted advertising rate $a_1(t)$. It seems reasonable to me that increases in advertising effectiveness would have diminishing effect as total advertising effort increased. In order to build a relationship it is necessary to estimate the amount of sales that would occur with no advertising support (S_{1n}) and the amount of sales that would occur with maximum advertising effort (S_{1m}). This relationship is graphed in Exhibit 3.1.1.

Exhibit 3.1 continued

Exhibit 3.1.1
Relationship between Adjusted Advertising Rate
and the Basic Advertising Effectiveness Index

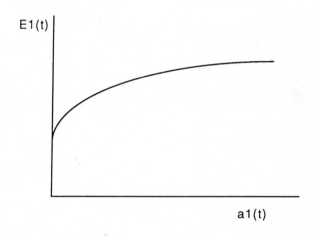

When the three advertising submodel variables $(h_1(t),\ k_1(t),\ X_1(t))$ are maintained at their standard values, $a_1(t)$ should be 1 and $E_1(t)$ should also be 1.

There is another effect that cannot be overlooked. Long after people have forgotten the original advertisements, they may be buying the brand as a result of having heard or seen the ads. This long term carry-over effect has been built into the model by adjusting the period's basic advertising effect index the same way the advertising rate was adjusted for memory. Here the adjusted advertising effect index $e_1(t)$ is:

$$e_1(t) = C_1 \times e_1(t-1) + (1-C_1) \times E_1(t)$$

where:

C_1 = carry-over effect of advertising per period.

Exhibit 3.1 continued

Salesforce Submodel

The salesforce submodel is identical in form to the advertising submodel, just the nature of the values are changed.

$$A_2(t) = \frac{h_2(t)}{h_{2o}} \times \frac{k_2(t)}{k_{2o}} \times \frac{X_2(t)}{X_{2o}}$$

where, for the salesforce submodel:
$X_2(t)$ = Salesforce budget in period t.
$h_2(t)$ = Coverage efficiency (calls per dollar).
$k_2(t)$ = Salesperson's effectiveness per call.
$A_2(t)$ = Unadjusted salesforce – effort rate
h_{2o} = Reference coverage efficiency
k_{2o} = Reference salesperson's effectiveness
X_{2o} = Reference salesforce budget

This index can also be adjusted for memory effect:

$$a_2(t) = B_2 \times A_2(t - 1) + (1 - B_2) \times A_2(t)$$

where:
$\qquad B_2$ = memory constant, fraction of last period's effort carried forward to the next period.

The relationship between $a_2(t)$ and the basic salesforce effect index $E_2(t)$ is hypothesized to be nonlinear and similar to the relationship in Exhibit 3.1.1. Once $E_2(t)$ is derived it can be adjusted for a long-term effect of the salesforce efforts (called the loyalty effect). In order to estimate this relationship it was necessary to estimate sales with no salesforce activity (S_{2n}) and with maximum salesforce activity (S_{2m}).

$$e_2(t) = C_2 \times e_2(t - 1) + (1 - C_2) \times E_2(t)$$

where:

$\qquad C_2$ = carry-over (loyalty effect).

Exhibit 3.1 continued

Price Submodel

The price submodel is much simpler than the previous two models. The relative price is first adjusted for inflationary factors.

$$a_3(t) = \frac{P_3(t)}{R_{p3}(t)}$$

where:

$R_{p3}(t)$ = Standard price adjusted each period to reflect inflation.

$P_3(t)$ = Price to be used in period t.

I would expect sales to follow OTC's demand curve. I tried to build in a functional relationship between price and sales which I felt reflects the elasticity of demand over a reasonable range of prices. That relationship is illustrated in Exhibit 3.1.2.

Exhibit 3.1.2
Relationship between Price $a_3(t)$
and Long-Term Sales Effects $e_3(t)$

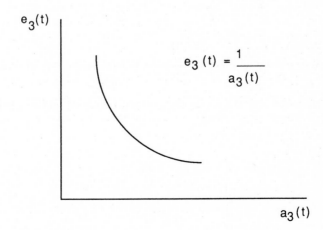

$$e_3(t) = \frac{1}{a_3(t)}$$

Exhibit 3.1 continued

The relationship that I have assumed is as follows:

$$e_3(t) = \frac{1}{a_3(t)}$$

Other Effects

There are a lot of other factors that could be included in our model. As I stated before, I feel that we should try to keep this model as simple as possible. Therefore, I have only included two other components, seasonality and category sales trend. I have used past historical data to derive standard quarterly indices. Exhibit 3.1.3 shows those indices. These numbers can be entered directly as Q_1 to Q_4 in the seasonality submodel.

Exhibit 3.1.3
Seasonality Indices

Quarter	Index
1	1.45
2	.75
3	.60
4	1.20

The final component I have included is category growth trend. It seems foolish to me to think that we can ignore changes that are impacting upon the entire category. Therefore, I have taken the past few years' category sales and forecasted the change in sales. The formula I have used starts with 1.0 for the first year's category sales and then changes according to the following formula:

$$e_5(t) = e_5(t - 1) \times (1 + g_5)$$

where:

$$g_5 = \text{growth rate}$$

Exhibit 3.1 continued

This then is an overview of the model I have developed. It has been loaded onto a spreadsheet file called **Markmix** on the attached disk and a printout of the spreadsheet is attached [see a copy of Gary's attachment in Section 3.2]. I suggest you play with it for awhile and get back to me with suggested refinements.

Maureen started to play with the model to get a feel for the kinds of things it would do. The first part of the model she examined was the price submodel. She raised the price from $2.49 to $2.79 to see if they made any more profit at year end. She found the contributions to profit went down. She then lowered the price to $1.99 and found that the contributions to profit went up. She kept lowering the price to observe the impact on profit. Much to her surprise the profits continued to rise even after she lowered the price below the brand's variable cost. Obviously the model was still too simple to be useful and had to take into account some other important factors. She sent a memo to Gary with a list of factors that she felt were relevant to the development of the price submodel (Exhibit 3.2).

Exhibit 3.2

To: Gary Norwood, Supervisor, M.R.D
From: Maureen Barnett, B.M. Feelgood
Re: Markmix Model

The price submodel has a few bugs in it still. It appears I neglected to give you some important facts necessary to develop the model. Could you incorporate the factors listed below.

a. The brand is a nationally advertised headache remedy. Most of the retailers have their own brand priced anywhere from 50 percent to 70 percent lower in price per tablet. They generally only stock Feelgood because of the demand created by the national advertising which reinforces its reputation as a safe, effective, high quality product. The retailers therefore usually sell Feelgood at the suggested retail price rather than lower the price to compete with their lower-priced house brands. We can therefore set the retail price and be reasonably sure the retailers will follow our guidelines.

Exhibit 3.2 continued

b.   The wholesalers and retailers insist they receive the standard markup on this product. The standard markup amounts to 45 percent of the retail price. In other words, we can set our (manufacturer's) price to be 55 percent of the retail price.

c.   In any case, we will not sell Feelgood for a price lower than its variable cost. If the retailers insist on a 45 percent markup then the lowest retail price possible should be at least 82 percent above our prevailing variable cost.

d.   Retail sales data indicate that the three nationally advertised headache remedies have 47 percent of the national market. The remaining market share is split among the many retail brands. All three national brands are priced at the same level. OTC is not viewed as the price leader so the other two brands will not likely follow our lead if we raise our price. This means we have a kinked demand curve, common to firms in an oligopolistic situation.

Exhibit 3.3

To: Maureen Barnett, B.M. Feelgood
From: Gary Norwood, Supervisor, M.R.D.
Re: Markmix Model Revisions

Based on your notes I made the following changes:

1. I started by assuming our variable cost set a lower limit on our manufacturer's price. I next assumed that retailers would continue to use a 45 percent margin. This means that our price decision at the factory determines the eventual retail price used in the model.

Exhibit 3.3 continued

2. I had to make several changes to the spreadsheet. I started by inserting a line in the extra information section and labelling it "Trial Manf. Price." I then changed the "Manufacturer's Price" line to accept the trial price unless it was less than 82 percent above our prevailing variable cost. If the trial price selected is too low to allow for the 45 percent margin the program prints the message "TOO LOW" in the "Manufacturer's Price" line. Make sure that you only enter prices in the "Trial Manf. Price" line from now on.

3. Next, I changed the retail price line so that it gives a 45 percent margin to the channel members.

4. I then tackled the effect of price $a_3(t)$ changes on sales $e_3(t)$. If prices are above the standard price (that is, $a_3(t)$ is greater than 1) then there will be a rapid decline in sales, which is indicated by the price effect index $e_3(t)$. I assumed a straight line relationship and slope of -3. This yields the equation $e_3(t) = 4 - 3a_3(t)$. If you feel the slope is too steep then feel free to edit the equation.

If the price is below the standard price then I assumed the old relationship $(e_3(t) = 1/a_3(t))$ still holds true. When you obtain more information to confirm your hypothesis concerning sales gained from retail brands I can change the equation to better reflect the true relationship.

With these changes to the model Maureen could again examine the potential impact of price changes on profits. Make these changes to your model and save the revised model on your own data disk. Remember to copy the changes made in the first period to all periods.

a. What did she discover about the profitability of price changes?

b. Is this a reasonable conclusion?

c. What further information would she need to properly design the submodel?

d. How would she obtain the information?

3.1.3 Marketing Mix Impact Model

Outputs from Submodels and Inputs to
Marketing Effectiveness Indices

Sales Influences	1988 Jan-Mar	1988 April-Jun	1988 Jul-Sept	1988 Oct-Dec
Variables				
e1 Advertising	1.00	1.00	1.00	1.00
e2 Salesforce Activity	1.00	1.00	1.00	1.00
e3 Price	1.00	1.00	1.00	1.00
e4 Seasonality	1.45	0.75	0.60	1.20
e5 Category Sales Trend	1.00	1.00	0.99	0.99

Additional Effectiveness Indices
for Direct Input if Desired

	1988 Jan-Mar	1988 April-Jun	1988 Jul-Sept	1988 Oct-Dec
e6 Consumer Promotion				
e6.1 Price-off	1.00	1.00	1.00	1.00
e6.2 Coupons	1.00	1.00	1.00	1.00
e6.3 Premiums	1.00	1.00	1.00	1.00
e6.4 Trade	1.00	1.00	1.00	1.00
e7 Product	1.00	1.00	1.00	1.00
e8 Package				
e8.1 Graphics	1.00	1.00	1.00	1.00
e8.2 Function	1.00	1.00	1.00	1.00
e8.3 Assortment	1.00	1.00	1.00	1.00
e9 Production Capacity	1.00	1.00	1.00	1.00
e10 Other Product Factors	1.00	1.00	1.00	1.00
e11 Other Environmental Fac	1.00	1.00	1.00	1.00
e12 Retail Activities				
e12.1 Availability	1.00	1.00	1.00	1.00
e12.2 Promotion	1.00	1.00	1.00	1.00
e12.3 Advertising	1.00	1.00	1.00	1.00
e12.4 Consumer Sales at Fixed Distribution	1.00	1.00	1.00	1.00
e13 Other Retail Factors	1.00	1.00	1.00	1.00

Additional Information Needed for
Marketing Mix Impact Model

	1988 Jan-Mar	1988 April-Jun	1988 Jul-Sept	1988 Oct-Dec
Budgeted Ad. & S.F. Exp	$1,471	$1,471	$1,471	$1,471
Manufacturer's Price	$1.38	$1.38	$1.38	$1.38
Variable Cost	$0.55	$0.55	$0.55	$0.55

Output From the Model

	1988 Jan-Mar	1988 April-Jun	1988 Jul-Sept	1988 Oct-Dec
Predicted Sales (Units)	7,250	3,731	2,970	5,910
Predicted Sales ($,000)	$10,005	$5,149	$4,099	$8,156
Predicted Contib. to FC	$6,018	$3,097	$2,465	$4,906
Adv. and Salesforce Exp.				$10,603
Actual Sales	0	0	0	0

Submodel Inputs
Advertising Submodel

So Reference Sales	5,000			
Xo Ref. Adv. Exp.	$1,121			
ho Ref. Media Efficiency	3.4			
ko Ref. Copy Effectiveness	1.00			

	1988 Jan-Mar	1988 April-Jun	1988 Jul-Sept	1988 Oct-Dec
X1t Advertising Expenditure	$1,121	$1,121	$1,121	$1,121
h1t Media Efficiency	3.4	3.4	3.4	3.4
k1t Copy Effectiveness	1.00	1.00	1.00	1.00
B1 Memory Effect	0.30	0.30	0.30	0.30
C1 Advertising Carry-over	0.50	0.50	0.50	0.50
S1n No Ads Sales Level	1,000	1,000	1,000	1,000
S1m Maximum Ads Sales Level	7,500	7,500	7,500	7,500
A1t Advertising Rate (AR)	1.00	1.00	1.00	1.00
a1t AR Adjusted for Memory	1.00	1.00	1.00	1.00
E1t Unadjusted Advertising Index	1.00	1.00	1.00	1.00
e1t Adv Effect Index	1.00	1.00	1.00	1.00

Salesforce Submodel

X2o Ref S.F. Exp. (000)	$350
h2o Ref. Coverage	0.01
k2o Ref. Call Eff.	1.00

	1988 Jan-Mar	1988 April-Jun	1988 Jul-Sept	1988 Oct-Dec
X2t Salesforce Budget	$350	$350	$350	$350
h2t Coverage Effectiveness	0.01	0.01	0.01	0.01
k2t Call Effectiveness	1.00	1.00	1.00	1.00
B2 Memory Effect	0.30	0.30	0.30	0.30
C2 Loyalty Effect	0.80	0.80	0.80	0.80
S2n No Salesforce Sales	1,000	1,000	1,000	1,000
S2m Max. Salesforce Sales	6,000	6,000	6,000	6,000
A2t Salesforce Rate (SR)	1.00	1.00	1.00	1.00
a2t SR Adjusted for Memory	1.00	1.00	1.00	1.00
E2t Unadj. S.F. Effect	1.00	1.00	1.00	1.00
e2t S.F. Effect Index	1.00	1.00	1.00	1.00

Price Submodel

T3o Price Trend (% increase every three months) 1.00 percent

	1988 Jan-Mar	1988 April-Jun	1988 Jul-Sept	1988 Oct-Dec
Rp3t Reference Price	$2.49	$2.51	$2.54	$2.57
P3t Feelgood Retail Price	$2.49	$2.51	$2.54	$2.57
a3t Price Rate	1.00	1.00	1.00	1.00
e3t Price Effect Index	1.00	1.00	1.00	1.00

Seasonality Submodel

Q1 First Quarter Index	1.45
Q2 Second Quarter Index	0.75
Q3 Third Quarter Index	0.60
Q4 Fourth Quarter Index	1.20

Category Sales Trend Submodel

G5o Category Growth (% change every 3 months) -0.50 percent

	1988 Jan-Mar	1988 April-Jun	1988 Jul-Sept	1988 Oct-Dec
e5t Category Trend Effect	1.00	1.00	0.99	0.99

3.2   Feelgood Headache Remedy (B)

Near the end of the 1988 fiscal year it had become apparent that sales of most OTC products were below forecast levels and OTC was short of cash. Word came down from upper management that budgets would be slashed for a year in order to maximize cash flow. In particular, it was felt that a one-year reduction in advertising expenditures would not substantially affect revenues from older brands but could help conserve needed cash in the short run. The cuts were to take effect January 1989 for up to one year.

Brand managers were permitted to present arguments against cuts, keeping in mind that upper management was unsympathetic to long-run concerns given the short-term crises facing the firm. Maureen felt she could test the effect of the cuts on profits using the model. She realized that the model did not measure cash flows directly but felt that the profit measure was a relatively close approximation for the present.

She first estimated the yearly contribution toward profit if all advertising were eliminated and found there was a drop in profit. She then built up the advertising budgets for the four periods of 1989 until she reached a point where contribution to profit dropped. She felt she had established that a total elimination of advertising would hurt rather than help cash flow.

She also felt there might be room for improvement in profit if the seasonality of sales was taken into consideration. This would mean advertising more during the period of heavy sales, and less during the period of low sales. Another option was to advertise based on estimated sales in the next period. This would mean more advertising in periods prior to heavy sales periods so that Feelgood would be in people's mind during the periods of heavy sales.

Finally, Maureen had heard that pulses of advertising were more economical than continuous advertising. This would suggest she advertise in one period followed by one or more periods of no advertising, then repeat the cycle. The question was, what was a reasonable time between heavy advertising periods and how much should she advertise in those periods?

Test the sensitivity of contribution to profits to changes in advertising as Maureen did and then test the three approaches to advertising to see if profits can be improved.

a.   What, according to the model, is the optimum allocation of advertising dollars in 1989?

b.   Is her use of the model at this stage appropriate?

c. What model assumptions/values affect the results of her analysis?

d. Should upper management agree to continue advertising the Feelgood brand based on her analysis?

3.3 Changing the Model

This section was created to remind you of some of the basic commands necessary to play with the model. We will also give you some hints on how to make the changes Maureen has to make. Please note, however, that this is not the assignment. You should make the changes to the model you feel are appropriate based on your analysis of the case.

3.3.1 Getting into the Model

The model cannot be accessed by running disk 1. Instead, you should boot a *Lotus*-compatible spreadsheet program and then load the spreadsheet called MARKMIX stored on disk 1.

When it is loaded it should automatically go to the menu area of the spreadsheet. If this does not happen, type *Alt M* (press the Alt key and the M key at the same time). You should then see the menu listed below. Alt M will always return you to the menu.

Marketing Mix Impact Model

Alt M   Takes you to this menu

Alt B   Beginning of the model

Alt I   Additional indices

Alt E   Extra information that is needed

Alt O   Ouputs from the model

Alt A   Advertising submodel

Alt S   Salesforce submodel

Alt P   Price submodel

Alt Q   Seasonality submodel (Quarterly index)

Alt T   Sales trend submodel

The other options listed are for your convenience in moving around the model. For instance, if you were interested in investigating the price component of the model, simply pressing Alt P would take you there directly.

3.3.2   Some Hints

1. Add rows by pressing the command key / followed by W, I, R, and return (row 53 should be a good place to do this).

2. In order to make the manufacturer's price conditional upon the variable costs use an @IF command. For instance, typing @IF(E53 >= 1.82 * E55,E53,"TOO LOW") into E54 (assuming you added the row at 53 and labelled it "Trial Manf. Price") should make sure the program only runs when the trial price is set high enough above the variable cost.

3. The retail price can be made dependent upon the manufacturer's price by setting it equal to the manufacturer's price divided by (1 − 0.55).

4. The price effect index can also be made conditional by using the @IF command. That is, if the price is above the reference price, have the index computed using one formula; otherwise have it use the second formula given.

5. Make sure you replicate all your changes across the entire model.

Chapter 4

THE BASICS OF SAMPLING

4.1   The Accuracy of Mean Estimates

To make inferences involving means you must use estimates of the standard deviation of the mean. The relationship between the standard deviation of a sample and the standard deviation of the mean estimates is often confused. The purpose of this program is to help you see the difference between the two and to help you understand the relationship among estimates of the two statistics and sample size. An example will be used to help illustrate these relationships.

4.1.1   Speedway Bus Lines

Speedway Bus Lines was faced with the possibility of cutting back their commuter services due to a lack of funding. The firm's fleet of buses needed to be replaced and the number and type of buses ordered depended on the amount of commuter services they would offer. Management also had the option of applying for state and federal grants to provide financial support for commuter services. The firm prided itself on the fact that it was a private company that derived most of its funding from passenger revenue and felt it should test public opinion on the issue of subsidies to support commuting services.

A marketing research firm was asked to conduct a survey in order to determine people's attitudes. Three variables were felt to be particularly important to the management. These were:

1. Whether people liked using the buses to commute.

2. How often they used the bus line for commuting.

3. Whether people were for or against government subsidization of the bus line so that it could continue providing special commuter bus services.

Assume for the moment that the distributions of the true values for these variables are as graphed in Exhibits 4.1–4.3. These are the distributions that would result from surveying every member of the population and graphing their responses. Exhibit 4.1 shows the distribution of attitudes toward using the bus line for commuting.

Exhibit 4.1
Distribution of Attitudes
Toward the Use of
Buses for Commuting

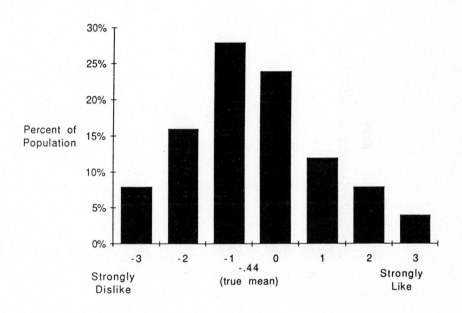

The mode is -1 and most people are negative toward commuting by bus. Responses appear to be normally distributed around the mode.

Exhibit 4.2 shows how often people used the commuter service (round trip) in the past month.

Exhibit 4.2
Number of Times the Bus Line Was Used
for Round Trip Commuting in April 1986

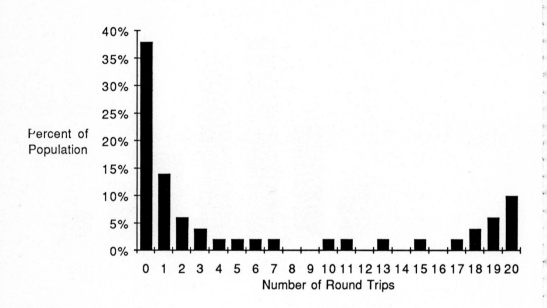

(6.18 = true mean)

Roughly 40 percent of the population never used the bus line for round-trip commuting in April. If April is representative, the users tend to either use the bus for commuting occasionally (1–6 times per month) or frequently (15–20 times a month).

Exhibit 4.3 shows the population's attitudes toward government subsidization of the bus line's commuter services.

Exhibit 4.3

Approval of Government
Subsidy for Commuter Bus Services

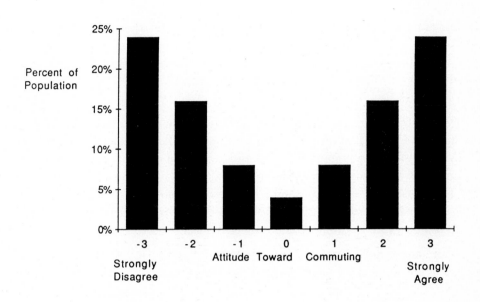

The population is obviously divided over the issue with half approving
the subsidy of the commuter services while half disapprove. They also very
strongly agree or disagree which results in responses concentrating at the
extremes of the scale.

4.1.2   Estimating Frequency Distributions

Assuming random unbiased samples are drawn from the population, as the
sample size increases the distributions of sample responses should more
closely resemble the actual distributions. To see what sample sizes are
required to approximate the population distributions, run part A of the
program "Mean Estimates" on the disk. Start with very small sample sizes
for each distribution and decide at what point larger sample sizes would be

a waste of money if you were trying to estimate the distribution for these variables.

4.1.3   Distribution of Mean Estimates

Now assume you wish to estimate the mean values for these three variables. To do this we would use sample data, but the question is, what sample size is appropriate? The answer depends on how accurate you want your estimate to be. The accuracy of your estimate will improve as your sample size increases.

To illustrate, run part B of the program "Mean Estimates" and select a sample size for the first variable. The computer will then select two hundred samples of the size you have specified and graph the distribution of the mean estimates over the distribution for the total population so that you can see the relationship. Start with a very small sample size of 2 or 3. Work your way up to sample sizes of 200 to 500. We do not recommend you try very large samples (for example, 10,000) as they take eons to run.

You should notice two things. First, the distribution of the mean estimates is normally distributed around the true mean. Since the distribution is based on only 200 mean estimates there is some chance it will not appear perfectly normal. However, if an infinite number of mean estimates were generated and graphed, the distribution would appear perfectly normal. Second, the variance of the mean estimates is considerably less than the variance for the whole population.

There is a third phenomenon which may not be apparent from your simulations. As sample size increases the improvement in accuracy, as measured by the reduced standard deviation of the estimates, is at first rapid. After a while substantial increases in sample size are required to obtain any significant improvement in accuracy.

Do these relationships hold true if the variable's variance is much higher, or its distribution is not normal? Try various sample sizes on the other two variables to see what effect the variable's distribution has on these relationships. You should find that, if the sample size is over 30, the distribution of the mean estimates again seems normal and has a much smaller standard deviation than the variable itself.

4.1.4 Sampling Distribution of the Means

In fact the relationship between a variable's standard deviation and the standard deviation of the mean estimates is:

$$S_{\bar{x}} = \frac{S_x}{\sqrt{n}}$$

where

$S_{\bar{x}}$ = the standard deviation of the mean estimates
S_x = the standard deviation of the sample data
n = the completed sample size

To test this equation do part C of the program. It will derive twenty estimates of the standard deviation of mean estimates based on twenty different sample standard deviations. It will then derive the actual standard deviation of the mean estimates to allow comparison between the 20 estimates and the actual. Note that as the sample size increases the estimates are more consistent.

4.1.5 Determining Accuracy

Now, how do you use this to determine the accuracy of your estimates? Going back to our example, let us assume it will cost $1,500 to develop and analyze the survey and $5.00 per completed interview. A sample of 400 would therefore cost $3,500. The bus line obviously won't spend $70,000 to do 20 of these surveys in order to estimate the standard deviation of the estimates; they will do just one. But then how can the researcher estimate the accuracy of the mean estimate derived from the one survey?

The survey will provide:

- $\bar{X}$—the sample mean.

- n—the completed sample size.

- S_x—the standard deviation of the sample.

- $S_{\bar{x}} = \frac{S_x}{\sqrt{n}}$—the standard deviation of the mean estimates.

One other factor is required to determine the accuracy of the estimate, $\bar{X}$. That is, that the distribution of the mean estimates is normal, and the area contained within different numbers of standard deviations about the mean is the same for all normal curves.

- That means that if we drew a large number of samples, approximately 68 percent of the mean estimates will fall within ± 1 standard deviation of the true mean.

- Furthermore, 95 percent of the mean estimates will fall within ± 2 standard deviations of the true mean.

You can test this by doing part D of the program. Once you specify a sample size, the program will generate the mean of 200 samples, calculate the mean and standard deviation of the mean estimates, calculate the number of means within the first one and two standard deviations and graph the results. If your sample size is large enough, the number of mean estimates within a given number of the standard deviations should correspond closely to a given percentage listed above.

4.1.6   Confidence Interval

The sample data provides only one estimate of the mean $(\bar{X})$. We know the chances of this estimate being exactly the same as the true mean are small. However, we know the probability of it being within a certain number of standard deviations of the true mean M (see Exhibit 4.4).

Exhibit 4.4

Distribution of Unbiased Mean Estimates
around the True Mean

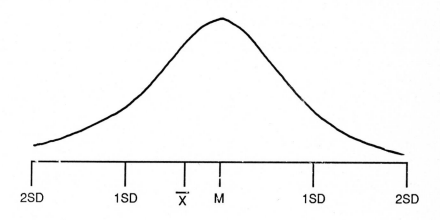

Conversely, we also know the probability of the true mean (M) being so many standard deviations from the estimate $\bar{X}$ since the two probabilities are the same. (If there is only a one in twenty chance the estimate will fall more than two standard deviations away from the true mean there must be a one in twenty chance that the true mean is within two standard deviations of the mean estimate $\bar{X}$.) We can therefore use the standard deviation of the mean estimates to determine the likelihood the true mean is within a specified number of standard deviations from the estimate.

In practice researchers specify a confidence level which indicates how confident they are the true mean will fall within a specific range of values above or below the derived estimate. The confidence level, in turn, determines the number of standard deviations to be used in specifying the confidence interval.

As a final exercise, do part E of the program. Here you specify the sample size and the computer will assume a 90 percent confidence level is desired and generate 20 mean estimates and the confidence interval for each. You can then determine how many times the true mean falls outside the confidence interval. Given 20 samples and a confidence level of 90 percent ($\pm$ 1.64 standard deviations), on the average the true mean should fall outside the confidence interval twice.

This last exercise should illustrate that you can never say for sure that the true mean is within the confidence interval (unless there are upper and lower bounds to the variable's values). Instead you can say the true mean will probably fall into the confidence interval for the percentage of times specified by your confidence level.

4.2 Random Sample Number Generator

The purpose of a random sample number generator is to generate random numbers that can be used for selecting sample elements.

The program generates random numbers and then sorts them into ascending order. You specify whether you want to generate single numbers or pairs of numbers and the computer will generate them within the range or ranges you specify.

As an example, assume you want to generate 100 random numbers in order to sample from an up-to-date list of 30,000 magazine subscribers. When asked for the low and high values you would input *1* and *30,000* respectively. The computer will first generate the numbers and then sort them. You will then have the choice of printing them on screen or directly to a printer.

The computer samples numbers with replacement. That means it is possible for the computer to select a number more than once. When your range of possible values is small relative to your sample size you may wish to generate more random numbers in order to allow for duplicates.

Sometimes you will want to generate pairs of random numbers if you will be sampling at two stages or levels. For example, if you want to select a sample of 500 telephone numbers from a telephone book that has 625 pages and 200 lines per page, you might ask for 500 pairs of random numbers (see the exercise following to find out why you might ask for more than 500). For the first level you specify a range of 1 to 625 in order to generate a sample of pages. For the second level you would specify a range of 1 to 200 to select the line number.

The output will look like this:

1. 2,187
2. 4,22
3. 17,76
4. 17,102
5. 24,157
⋮
500. 622,5

When the same number is generated more than once at the first level (see number pairs 3 and 4) the number pairs are ordered according to the second level numbers. The program generates a maximum of 9,999 random numbers or number pairs.

4.2.1   Sampling from the Telephone Book

Assume you are conducting a telephone survey of the local metropolitan area and require 500 completed surveys. You would be using the random sample number generator program to select the numbers, but you would have to generate more than 500 pairs of numbers in order to compensate for lines that will not be usable and residential listings that will not yield completed interviews.

The first step in selecting a sample from the telephone book is to decide which sections of the book you will include in your sample list. There may be sections of the book listing communities outside your defined population. Once you have selected the sections to be included on the sample list you should sum the number of pages in these sections. If there were 752 pages you would set the first level range to be 1 to 752.

Next count the number of lines per column using the edge of a paper to mark off every fifth line. If there are 200 lines (4 columns of 50 lines) then the second level values will range from 1 to 200. If the line number 132 is generated you would select the 32nd line in third column using the paper edge as a guide.

Not every line will generate a usable number. You will have to generate extra numbers to allow for:

1. Business numbers — 30–40 percent of the lines could be for business listings. You should not simply select the next residential number above or below this listing since the owners tend to be listed next to their business.

2. Residential listings that require more than one line — People with long names or long addresses may require two or more lines for their listing. They have a much higher chance of being sampled so you should decide on a selection rule, such as selecting them only if you pick the line that contains their telephone number.

3. Headings and empty spaces.

4. Children's telephone numbers — People that have a separate children's telephone tend to be on the upper end of the socio-economic scale. Be sure to select the main number for the household. Decide on a rule as for multiple line listings.

Exercise A

As an exercise, take your local telephone book and select the sections you feel would represent the market for a large furniture store located downtown. Use the program to generate 50 pairs of numbers for selection of lines. Using the sample you have generated fill in the table below. Save your printout of random numbers to hand in.

	Percent of Lines
Business numbers	_____
Extra residential lines	_____
Headings or empty spaces	_____
Childrens' phones	_____
Other nonqualifying lines	_____
Usable lines	_____
Total	100%

You now have an estimate of the percentage of usable lines. For illustration, assume you found that roughly 50 percent of the lines have a usable residential listing. This means that in order to obtain the desired 500 telephone numbers you would have to double the number of number pairs generated $(500/.5 = 1000)$.

However, not all of these numbers will result in a completed survey. You will have to take into account:

1. Not-in-service numbers — Some of the residential numbers listed may no longer be in service since people have moved. The percentage of numbers not in service may be as high as 5 percent when the telephone book is published and may reach 15 percent after a year, depending on the mobility of people in the community. If the telephone book has

been out for 6 months we might assume 90 percent of the numbers are still in service.

2. Nonresponse — There will be people you can't reach because they are not at home when you call. Past experience may indicate that after three attempts you will reach approximately 80 percent of the households.

3. Refusals — Even when you reach a household you may be refused permission to conduct the survey. The refusal rate tends to vary substantially among communities so if it is possible you should estimate this figure based on the experience of researchers. We will assume that 90 percent of those reached will not refuse to participate.

These three factors would reduce your percentage of usable numbers to 65 percent ($.8 \times .9 \times .9 = .648$) of the usable numbers identified. When combined with the effect of unusable lines, you would have to generate approximately 1,500 pairs of numbers ($500/(.5 \times .65) = 1,538$).

Exercise B

Using the percentage of usable lines you found in exercise A, and the percentages assumed above, estimate how many number pairs would have to be generated to arrive at a completed sample of 300.

A final note: Once a sample is generated you should attempt to reach all the households selected. If you stop when you reach your target number of completed surveys you may be introducing bias into the results. People living in communities listed at the end of the telephone book may be missed, as might be people whose last name starts with a letter near the end of the alphabet. One solution is to generate fewer numbers than you feel you really need. Then if you have a higher rate of completed surveys than expected you will not have to waste time and money surveying the whole list to minimize the risk of bias. If you fall short of the needed number of completed surveys, it is relatively easy to generate a small sample to obtain a few more.

Chapter 5

DETERMINING SAMPLE SIZE

5.1   Sample Size Analysis

Introduction

This program allows you to quickly determine the required sample size for a simple random sample assuming you will perform specific types of analyses on the data once it is collected. The advantages of the program over pencil and paper are the immediate availability of the variety of formulas you might use and, of course, the speed of calculations. These advantages are important when determining the required sample size for two reasons. First, many types of analyses are likely to be performed in one set of data and the required sample size for each analysis and each variable should be considered before the final sample size is selected. Second, the speed of calculation allows you to test the sensitivity of the derived sample size to changes in important values such as the desired precision, confidence level and estimated standard deviation. It may be found that a small but acceptable decrease in desired precision could substantially reduce the required sample size.

To make use of this program as a learning tool you should go through the questions at the end of this section. When entering your values see if you can guess what the required sample size will be. Then go back and make some changes to the input values to determine their impact on the required sample size. This will help you understand the impact of varying these values. For example, you might go back and enter different estimates of the standard deviation. If you found the required sample size was relatively insensitive to these changes then you would not recommend a pretest if its main purpose was to estimate the population's standard deviation.

Before using this program you should read the appropriate sections of your text so that you understand the principles involved. Since most texts cover the estimation of means and proportions, using either absolute or relative precision, these methods are the first two options available to you. The next four options (3 through 6) may not be discussed in your text but are fairly self-explanatory and are required frequently in practice. The program will first give you the choice of six methods of determining the appropriate sample size (Screen 1).

Screen 1

```
                    Sample Size Estimation

        Select a Method of Calculating the Sample Size.

    A. When estimating proportions.
    B. When estimating means.
    C. When testing for hypothesized proportions.
    D. When testing for hypothesized means.
    E. When testing for differences in proportions
       derived from two segments.
    F. When testing for differences in means
       derived from two segments.
    Q. Quit

            Select A – F, or Q
```

Select the desired method by typing in the appropriate letter. You can also leave the program at this point by entering *Q*. Each method is briefly described below to help you understand the terminology used in the programs.

5.1.1 Calculation of Sample Size in Estimation Problems Involving Proportions

A or R (Absolute or Relative Precision)

If you select this method you must first decide whether you will specify the allowable sampling error in absolute or relative terms by selecting *A* or *R*. Absolute precision involves stating precision in the units you are measuring, (for example, ±\$50 if you are measuring dollars, or ±0.05 if you are measuring a proportion). Relative precision is stated as a percentage of the sample mean or proportion (for example, ±10 percent of \$500 is the equivilant of ±\$50 in absolute terms and ±10 percent of the proportion 0.50 is the equivilant of ±0.05 in absolute terms).

P (Proportion)

When dealing with proportions, the standard deviation of the data is a function of the value of the proportion (P). The maximum standard deviation occurs when P = .50. It is relatively constant until P < .30 or P > .70 when it decreases rapidly. If you feel the true proportion is in the .01 to .30 or .70 to .99 range, it is important to specify this value. If you feel the true value is somewhere between .30 and .70, or if you have no idea at all, then specifying a value of .50 for P will give you the maximum sample required given your other input values.

E (Sampling Error)

If you selected absolute precision, you will have to input an absolute value (E) for the desired sampling error at the confidence level you will specify. For example, if you want to be able to say the confidence interval around your estimate is ± 5 percent at the 90 percent confidence level, then specify the proportion .05 as your desired level of sampling error. The required sample size is very sensitive to precision so be careful not to specify an unnecessarily high level.

R (Relative Error)

If you select relative precision you will have to input a relative value (R) for the desired sampling error at the confidence level you will specify. R is the proportion of P that you wish to set as your confidence interval. If you estimate the true proportion P to be .40 and you set R = .15, then your confidence interval will be ± .06.

CL (Confidence Level)

You have five degrees of confidence to choose from (99, 95, 90, 80, 70 percent). If you choose CL = 95 percent and E = .03, then you hope to be able to say, once your analysis is completed, that your estimate has a confidence interval of ± .03 at the 95 percent confidence level. You should not specify an unnecessarily high confidence level because this will substantially increase the required sample size and cause unnecessary costs.

Once you specify the confidence level (CL), the computer uses the corresponding Z value in its calculations.

Screen 2

```
                    Sample Size Estimation

Select (A)bsolute or (R)elative error level ?  A
Best estimate of the actual proportion ?  .5000
What is the maximum acceptable ABSOLUTE error (E)? ±  0.050
Estimated population size ?  10000


    Your desired level of confidence – Enter (1–5)  2
           1. 99% confident      Z = 2.47
           2. 95% confident      Z = 1.96
           3. 90% confident      Z = 1.64
           4. 80% confident      Z = 1.28
           5. 70% confident      Z = 1.04


         Use ↑ ↓ to move around. Press PgDn when done.
```

N (Population Size)

Very rough approximations are all that are required for this input value since the required sample size is independent of the population size until it is 5 percent or more of the population. If you know, for example, the number of households in a state or province is about one half million, input 500,000 as the value. Its effect will change very little if you input 400,000 or 600,000. It is only when the required sample size derived assuming an infinite population is 60 percent or more of the true population size that any degree of precision for N is necessary.

Most texts claim that N should be ignored if the derived sample size, assuming an infinite population, is less than 5 or 10 percent of the true population. This is based on the fact that the added analysis required to determine the appropriate sample size and estimate parameters once the data is collected is generally not warranted by the savings in sampling costs and reduced sampling error.

The computer, however, can quickly calculate sample size under both assumptions. If there is a substantial reduction in sampling error because of the population's size, remember to use the finite population correction factor when actually doing your analysis so that the confidence intervals you derive will be those you specified when determining the required sample size.

Screen 3

```
┌─────────────────────────────────────────────────────────────────┐
│                    Sample Size Estimation                         │
│                                                                   │
│       Assuming an infinite population size,                       │
│       you need a sample size of 384.                              │
│                                                                   │
│       However, the calculated sample size                         │
│       is 3.84% of the population.                                 │
│                                                                   │
│       This means that a sample size of                            │
│       only 370 is required.                                       │
│                                                                   │
│                                                                   │
│                                                                   │
│                                                                   │
│   Hit <ESC> to Return to main menu, Any other key to try again.   │
│                                                                   │
└─────────────────────────────────────────────────────────────────┘
```

Two required sample sizes may be reported (Screen 3). The first is based on the assumption that the population is infinite. If there is any reduction at all in the required sample size because of the population correction factor, then the second sample size will be reported.

5.1.2   Calculations of Sample Size in Estimation Problems Involving Means

The inputs for this program are basically the same as those required for the proportions program except that you are not restricted to proportions and you must specify an estimate for the population standard deviation.

SD (Standard Deviation)

This is the estimated standard deviation of the population. It can frequently be based on standard deviations derived from previous samples or from a pretest of the questionnaire. If you feel the population distribution is normal, then a value of 1/8 of the range of values can be input as a very rough approximation of the standard deviation. If you are unsure of the accuracy of your estimate, then input the lowest and highest values you feel are possible to determine the sensitivity of the required sample size to this estimate. If the range of required sample sizes is too large, then you may wish to do a pretest to derive a more accurate estimate.

5.1.3 Determination of Sample Size in Problems Involving Hypothesis Testing of Proportions

At this point the program does not calculate a required sample size assuming a finite population. Keep this in mind when doing your analysis.

Screen 4

```
                        Sample Size Estimation

                      Proportions can not equal 0 !

        What is P0 ?  [.5000]
        What is P1 ?  [.5800]
        Estimated population size ?  [10000]
        Select 1–5 for the α level ?  [4]
        Select 1–5 for the β level ?  [2]




            1. Error Probability of .01 ,Z = 2.32
            2. Error Probability of .05 ,Z = 1.64
            3. Error Probability of .10 ,Z = 1.28
            4. Error Probability of .20 ,Z = 0.84
            5. Error Probability of .30 ,Z = 0.52

            Use ↑ ↓ to move around.  Press PgDn when done.
```

For this analysis you will have to input five values. (See Screen 4.)

PO (Probability of Null Hypothesis)

This is the proportion associated with the null hypothesis (HO). If the null hypothesis is accepted (PO is the true population proportion), then no opinion is formed or no action is taken. This might be called the stop proportion. For example, if a company would definitely not introduce a new brand if the potential market share was .09 or less then PO would be set equal to .09.

P1 (Probability of Alternative Hypothesis)

This is the proportion associated with the alternate hypothesis (H1). If this hypothesis is accepted (P1 is the true population proportion), then the opinion would be formed, or the action taken. Usually this is the go proportion. For example, if the company needs .13 of the market to introduce a new brand, then P1 would be set to .13.

5.1.4   N (Population Size)

What was said previously is still true.

α (Alpha)

Alpha is the probability of making a type I error. That is, the probability of concluding the go ahead proportion P1 is true when in fact the stop proportion PO is true. For scientific research, alpha is generally set to .05 or .01. However, in market research it may be reasonable to set alpha to .20 or .10. This is because you don't always need to know for sure that a strategy will work, only that there is a very good probability (80 – 90 percent) that it will. That is, there is an 80 – 90 percent probability you will conclude P1 is correct when in fact PO is correct. Given your alpha level, the computer inserts the appropriate Z value into the equation.

β (Beta)

Beta is the probability of making a type II error. That is, the probability of concluding the stop proportion PO is true when in fact the go proportion P1 is true. Generally marketers do not wish to miss the chance to make a profit. If P1, the go proportion, is the true population value, they do not wish to conclude incorrectly that the PO is true and therefore that there is no marketing opportunity. You should consider setting this fairly low, at the most .10, probably .05 or .01. Given your beta level, the computer inserts the appropriate Z value into the equation.

5.1.5 Calculation of Sample Size for Hypothesis Testing Problems Involving Means

The inputs for this program are basically the same as those required for the proportions program except that you are not restricted to proportions and you must specify an estimate for the population standard deviation.

5.1.6 Calculation of Sample Size When Testing Differences in Proportions Derived from Two Segments

For this analysis you will have to input six values. These are:
Screen 5

Sample Size Estimation

Segment A is what proportion of the population (PA) ? .2000
Segment B is what proportion of the population (PB) ? .2500

The two proportions P1 & P2 whose difference you wish to test? P1 = .5000
P2 = .5800

Critical difference: P1 – P2 = -.08000
Estimated size of popoulation ? 10000

Your desired level of confidence – Enter (1–5) 2
1. 99% confident   Z = 2.47
2. 95% confident   Z = 1.96
3. 90% confident   Z = 1.64
4. 80% confident   Z = 1.28
5. 70% confident   Z = 1.04

Use ↑ ↓ to move around. Press PgDn when done.

PA (Proportion Segment A)

This is the estimated size of one of the segments to be analyzed. If segment A is estimated to be 15 percent of the population, the proportion is .15. Normally you would want to determine the required sample size using the two smallest segments. This would ensure that comparisons between all segments would be at least as accurate as you specified in this analysis. Sometimes you may not know the size of the segments, or even how many you will have. However, one can make assumptions. For example, it may be that any segment smaller than 10 percent of the population will not be worth a detailed examination, so you assume the smallest important segment will be 10 percent and the next smallest about 15 percent. If you know there will be four segments, then it is reasonable to assume the smallest will be about half the average size, or 12 percent.

PB (Proportion Segment B)

This is the estimated size of the second segment being analyzed. If different degrees of accuracy are required when comparing different segments, you should test for different combinations of segments and desired accuracies to observe their effect on the required sample size. See question 5.

P1 and P2 (Proportions P1 and P2 for Segments A and B)

You are actually specifying two important values here. The first is (P1 − P2) — the amount of sampling error you wish to allow given the confidence level you will specify. The second is the standard deviation associated with the segments. The standard deviation will be highest if P1 and P2 are near .5 and lowest if they are near 0 or 1.

CL (Confidence Level)

This is the level of confidence you will have that the sampling error is not greater than the amount (P1 − P2).

N (Population Size)

The computer will automatically calculate the required sample size assuming a finite population size and indicate the corrected sample size if it is less than the required sample size assuming an infinite population.

Note that the implied difference in proportions to be tested is listed as well. If this value is very small the computer may display the number in scientific notation such as 5E-03 which is .005 in standard notation.

When the sample size is determined the estimated sample sizes for the two segments you specified are also reported.

Screen 6

Sample Size Estimation

Assuming an infinite population size
the sample size required would be 1340.

This would mean sample sizes of
268 for segment A and
335 for segment B.

However, the calculated sample size
is 13.4% of the population.

This means that a sample size of
only 1182 is required.

This would mean sample sizes of
236 for segment A and
295 for segment B.

Hit <ESC> to Return to main menu, Any other key to try again.

5.1.7 Calculation of Sample Size When Testing for Differences in Means Derived from Two Segments

The inputs for this program are basically the same as those required for the proportions program except that you are not restricted to proportions and you must specify estimates for the segment standard deviations. The equation used for the test assumes different standard deviations for each segment. However, if they are the same, or you only know what the population standard error is, then put the same value in for each.

5.1.8   Assignment Questions

1. (a) A random sample is to be taken of households in the Miami-Fort Lauderdale area to determine the potential sales of a new service. The number of households is estimated to be 950,000. A small pretest found that 7 percent of the households were interested in the service. The firm desires an accuracy of 7 percent, ±2 percent at the 95 percent confidence level. Before doing any analysis, what sample size would you guess, given these figures, would be required? What size sample is required?

   (b) Suppose the sample extent was extended to cover all of the continental United States, with an estimated 86,000,000 households. What sample size would you guess would be required? What size sample is required?

2. (a) A random sample is to be taken of customer expenditures at a grocery store in order to estimate the average expenditure per visit of its customers. Paper tapes with the recorded values of each receipt given out in the last year are available for sampling of receipt values. It is estimated that approximately 4 million receipts were given to customers last year. A quick sampling of some of the values found on the tapes showed an average expenditure of about $30.00 and a standard deviation of about $34.00. The manager felt she needed a precise estimate, within ±2 percent of the mean at the 99 percent confidence level. What sample size would you guess would be required? What sample size is required?

   (b) What would be the required sample size if she decided the precision required was to be within ±5 percent of the mean at the 90 percent confidence level?

3. Suppose for the survey in question 1 the firm's management would definitely proceed with the service if 9 percent of the households were interested and would definitely not proceed if the interest was less than 6 percent. They felt there was a potential for high profits from the service so they wanted to be 95 percent sure they did not make a type II error; that is, conclude that less than 6 percent of the market was interested when in fact more than 9 percent was interested. They were, however, more willing to go after the market if it looked reasonably promising and therefore were willing to be only 80 percent confident

they would not make a type I error; that is, conclude the interest was 9 percent or better when there was a chance the interest was actually 6 percent or less. What is the required sample size?

4. Suppose that the manager of the store in question 2 would introduce a bingo card promotion if the average expenditure was $32.00 or more but would not if the expenditure was $28.00 or less. She wishes to be 90 percent certain she does not mistakenly conclude that the true average is $28.00 or less when it is possibly $32.00 or more. She wants to be 95 percent certain she does not mistakenly conclude the average is $32.00 or more when it is possibly $28.00 or less. What is the required sample size?

5. A random sample of the estimated 1.8 million car owners living in Virginia is to be taken in order to do a survey on motor oil purchase habits. The analysis will divide the sample into four segments based on where the respondents most frequently purchase their motor oil. The size of the segments is expected to be roughly:

Service Stations	45%
Automotive and Department Stores	30%
Grocery Stores	15%
Other Sources	10%

The study's main objective is to examine the potential of the Automotive and Department Store segment and the Grocery Store segment to respond to changes in the distribution and pricing elements of the marketing strategy. The Other Sources segment was deemed to be too small to be considered as a target market. The researchers will examine the segment, but less precision will be required.

The questions will focus on the customer's last purchase of motor oil. The important proportions to be estimated will be the proportion of times the respondents found more than one brand available, the proportion of times they switched to a new brand because the brand they preferred was not available and the proportion of times they claimed to have checked the prices before making the purchase.

The marketing managers had no idea what the true proportions were, but they did know they wanted to be able to detect differences of .08

between segments with 90 percent confidence. (A difference of .10 would be acceptable when comparing the Other Sources segment.) It was suggested that proportions around .50 (for example, P1 = .50 and P2 = .58) be assumed when determining the required sample size since that would be a worst-case scenario as far as the estimated population standard deviation was concerned.

(a) What is the required sample size? (Be sure to consider the sample size required to examine the Other Sources segment.)

(b) What would be the required sample size if it were assumed that P1 = .20 and P2 = .28? Why is it less? Is the use of P1 = .50 and P2 = .58 a reasonable way to determine the required sample size?

6. Suppose the firm in question 5 also wished to compare the average number of quarts purchased by the various segments. The overall average quarts per car owner purchased was approximately 8 quarts last year with a population standard deviation of 3.7 quarts. They want to be able to detect differences of about 1 quart with 90 percent confidence.

(a) What sample size is required to compare the number of quarts purchased by different segments?

(b) What will have the greatest impact on the required sample size?

   i. Increasing the desired confidence level to 95 percent.

   ii. Decreasing the critical difference to 0.5 quarts.

   iii. Estimating the population standard deviation to be 6.0.

7. What sample size would you aim for if you were taking a random sample of undergraduate students at your university to determine whether they were for or against an additional charge of $50.00 to pay for new computer facilities? The charge would be added to their regular tuition fees. Assume you will want to compare the responses of first-year students, second-year students and all other undergraduate students to see if the proportion of students against the increase differs among these student segments. What assumptions did you make?

8. A computer manufacturer is conducting two surveys to determine the potential interest in its market area for two models of a new computer

system designed to help firms process payrolls. Model A is a desktop computer designed for small businesses with 10 to 100 full-time employees while Model B is a floor unit designed for larger businesses with 101 to 500 employees. There are an estimated 20,000 small businesses and 200 larger businesses in the market. A pretest has already been conducted with the following results for those questions felt to be critical to the study.

		Small Businesses	Larger Businesses
		n=20	n=20
1. How many paychecks per month do you issue?	mean	40	320
	stand. dev.	31	280
2. Approximately how many man hours per month do you spend preparing the paychecks?	mean	35	102
	stand. dev.	18	49
3. Based on questions 1 & 2:			
Percent spending more than 30 minutes per paycheck.		31%	23%
4. Do you have a computerized system for payroll handling?	Yes	19%	47%
	No	81%	53%
5. In your opinion, will your firm be considering the purchase of a new computerized payroll system in the next three years?	Yes	25%	30%
	No	70%	60%
	No Idea	5%	10%

For all estimates a 90 percent confidence level was desired. The desired accuracies (all in absolute terms), were:

Question	Small Businesses	Larger Businesses
1	± 4	± 20
2	± 3	± 5
Derived from 1 & 2	± 3%	± 3%
3	± 5%	± 5%
4	± 5%	± 5%

What sample size would you recommend and why?

9. A budget of $20,000 has been allocated by the public relations department of a large service corporation to determine people's satisfaction with the corporation and whether there were enough problems with the quality of service being offered to significantly affect the public's image of the corporation. While several variables would be measured in the survey, the most important variables were:

   (a) The index of corporate satisfaction. This is a well-tested multivariate measure derived from eight questions asked during the survey. The responses to the eight questions are combined to provide a composite measure of respondents' satisfaction with the corporation. In the past the distribution of this variable has been normal about a mean of 31.56 with a standard deviation of 22.6. If the level of satisfaction fell below 28.00, then action would be taken to remedy the situation.

   (b) The proportion of the 4.5 million adults in the market who had had problems or complaints with any of the corporation's services in the past two years. If the proportion is greater than .10, then the corporation would conduct further research to determine the causes of the problems, invest in new quality-control systems and set up a complaint handling department. The people in PR were confident, however, that the actual proportion was less than .065.

   Three research firms had been asked to submit research proposals based on these specifications. All three firms would do the survey by telephone, but the sample sizes, costs, and response rates (percent of telephone numbers selected resulting in a completed interview), differed considerably.

   Firm A would have a completed sample size of 4,000 at a cost of $10,000. They expected a response rate of about 50 percent.

Firm B would have a completed sample size of 2,000 at a cost of $18,000. They expected a response rate of 75 percent.

Firm C would have a completed sample size of 600 at a cost of $12,000. They expected a response rate of 85 percent.

As the marketing manager you have been asked to help appraise the proposals. What would you recommend and why?

5.2   Stratified Sample Analysis

The purpose of this program is to help you determine the gain in statistical efficiency by using a proportionate stratified sampling procedure instead of a simple random sample. The program does this when your proposed analysis will be estimation of means and proportions.

5.2.1   Some Theory

A stratified sample occurs when a parent population has been divided into mutually exclusive and collectively exhaustive subsets (called strata) and a simple random sample is drawn independently from each subset or stratum. It is a proportionate stratified sample if the elements selected from the strata are selected in proportion to the relative number of elements in each stratum in the population. If a particular stratum has a quarter of the population's elements, then one quarter of a proportionate stratified sample's elements would come from that stratum.

You should consider a stratified sample if the important analysis will be limited to the calculation of means and frequencies or proportions. If you intend to use more sophisticated analysis techniques such as factor analysis or AID, then these analyses may require a larger sample size.

Statistical efficiency refers to the accuracy of your estimates for a given sample size. Accuracy is specified as the confidence interval (for example, ± 5 percent) at a particular confidence level (for example, the 90 percent confidence level). There will be increased statistical efficiency due to stratification:

1. the greater the difference in the proportions or means among the strata.

2. the less variance within each strata relative to the variance for the whole population.

3. the greater the number of strata used. (The program handles up to 16 strata.)

If you have identified characteristics that can be used to stratify a sample, and they are related to the variable of interest, then you should use this program to determine the relative efficiency of a stratified sample.

The statistical efficiency of the stratified sample can rise dramatically with an increase in the number of strata. Therefore, if the cost of stratification is not great, you should search for two or more variables that can be used in combination to form strata.

5.2.2   Program Input

You will first see Screen 1, shown below. Select *A* or *B* if you wish to specify the desired accuracy and receive the impact of stratified sampling on sample size. Select *C* or *D* if you wish to specify the sample size and receive the relative statistical efficiency of a stratified sample over a random sample.

Screen 1

```
┌──────────────────────────────────────────────────────────┐
│             Stratified Sample Impact Analysis             │
│       Select A,B,C,or D                                   │
│                                                           │
│       You specify the confidence interval and receive the │
│       suggested sample size and cost estimates as output. │
│                                                           │
│            A. Estimation of a mean                        │
│                                                           │
│            B. Estimation of a proportion                  │
│                                                           │
│       You specify the sample size and receive the probable│
│       confidence interval and standard deviation of the mean│
│       estimate as output.                                 │
│                                                           │
│            C. Estimation of a mean                        │
│                                                           │
│            D. Estimation of a proportion                  │
│                                                           │
└──────────────────────────────────────────────────────────┘
```

Regardless of your choice, you will next be asked to provide information about the strata. (The values you input are enclosed in the boxes.)

Screen 2

```
┌─────────────────────────────────────────────────────────┐
│   Stratified Sample Impact Analysis                       │
│                                                           │
│   How many strata will there be?  ┌─┐                     │
│                                   │4│                     │
│                                   └─┘                     │
│   What is the estimated population size?  ┌───────┐       │
│                                           │1000000│       │
│                                           └───────┘       │
│   What is your survey's fixed costs?  ┌────────┐          │
│                                       │$2000.00│          │
│                                       └────────┘          │
│   What is your survey's variable costs?  ┌──────┐         │
│                                          │$5.00 │         │
│                                          └──────┘         │
└─────────────────────────────────────────────────────────┘
```

First enter the number of strata you would form. The default value of 2 is already shown. This is also the minimum number of strata you can have. If you intend to have four strata, enter that number and use the down arrow to move to the next line. If you are stratifying on two dimensions of three categories each, you would end up with 9 strata and you should enter *9*. The maximum number of strata this program handles is 16.

You are then asked to indicate the population size. Only very rough estimates are required for this figure, unless you expect your sample size to be more than 60 percent of the population. If you are sampling adults in a city and the population is somewhere between 200,000 and 300,000, enter 250,000 as an approximation.

Next you must estimate the survey's fixed cost. This would include all costs associated with developing the questionnaire, survey design, analysis, and report generation. While this is an important component of the total cost, it is important for another reason. Often stratification may produce a substantial increase in statistical efficiency, but because fixed costs are relatively high compared to total variable costs the savings may be a small proportion of total costs. In such instances stratification may not be worth the effort.

The variable cost includes the cost of sample selection, questionnaire printing, interview time, postage, telephone, and travel. You may at any time use the up or down arrows to change your input values. When you are satisfied, hit the page down (PgDn) key to advance to the next screen.

If you are estimating a mean, the screen will look like this:

Screen 3

```
Stratified Sample Impact Analysis

STRATA    Estimated    Estimated             Proportionate
          Mean         Standard deviation    Size of stratum

1         450.00       50.00                  .250
2         230.00       35.00                  .350
3         125.00       40.00                  .400

Sum of Proportionate Sizes of Strata: 1.000

PgDn for next screen, Use ↑ ↓ to move around.
```

To use the program, you will have to estimate the means and standard deviations in advance. Estimates can come from the results of previous research or small pretests. Even educated guesses may be sufficient as input. If the results show substantial savings from using a stratified sample, a pretest to verify the guesses is probably justified.

If your analysis involves the estimation of proportions, you will only have to enter the estimated value of the proportion for each stratum and the estimated stratum size. If, for example, you are estimating the proportion of customers that might be interested in purchasing a product, you might estimate .80 (80 percent), .60 (60 percent), and .20 (20 percent) for three strata that you have defined and these strata make up 25 percent, 35 percent, and 40 percent of the population respectively. You would enter the data as illustrated on Screen 4.

Screen 4

```
┌──────────────────────────────────────────────────────────────────┐
│                                                                    │
│           Stratified Sample Impact Analysis                        │
│                                                                    │
│      STRATA    Estimated Value   Estimated Proportionate           │
│                in Stratum        Size of Stratum                    │
│                                                                    │
│        1          [.800]             [.250]                        │
│        2          [.600]             [.350]                        │
│        3          [.200]             [.400]                        │
│                                                                    │
│           Sum of Proportionate Sizes of Strata: 1.000              │
│                                                                    │
│       PgDn for next screen, Use ↑ ↓  to move around.               │
└──────────────────────────────────────────────────────────────────┘
```

If you selected A or B in Screen 1, you will be asked next to specify the desired confidence interval. The confidence is defined as a range around your estimate. If you are estimating a mean, then it can be any number greater than 0. If you are estimating a proportion, then you will have to specify a value between 0 and 1.

Screen 5

```
┌──────────────────────────────────────────────────────────────────┐
│          Stratified Sample Impact Analysis                         │
│                                                                    │
│  What is the desired confidence interval? ± [.050]                 │
│                                                                    │
└──────────────────────────────────────────────────────────────────┘
```

If you selected C or D, you will be asked to specify the desired sample size. Enter any number from 1-9999999 (although numbers near the number of strata may give you strange results).

Finally, in all cases, you must specify the desired confidence level before the program produces results (Screen 6).

Screen 6

```
┌─────────────────────────────────────────────────┐
│                                                   │
│         Stratified Sample Impact Analysis         │
│                                                   │
│  Please select your desired level of confidence (CL). │
│                                                   │
│                                                   │
│         1. 99% confident, Z = 2.47                │
│         2. 95% confident, Z = 1.96                │
│         3. 90% confident, Z = 1.64                │
│         4. 80% confident, Z = 1.28                │
│         5. 70% confident, Z = 1.04                │
│                                                   │
│                                                   │
│                                                   │
│                Select 1 - 5                       │
│                                                   │
└─────────────────────────────────────────────────┘
```

5.2.3 Program Output

If you selected A or B on Screen 1, the program reminds you of what you specified as the desired confidence interval at the specified confidence level. It then produces two sample size estimates and costs. The one set assumes a proportionate stratified sample, while the other assumes a simple random sample (Screen 7).

Screen 7

```
┌─────────────────────────────────────────────────┐
│         Stratified Sample Impact Analysis         │
│                                                   │
│   Confidence level specified: 95%                 │
│   Confidence interval specified: ±.05             │
│                                                   │
│   Assuming a stratified sample:                   │
│      Sample size required: 194                    │
│      Cost of survey: $2776                        │
│                                                   │
│   Assuming a random sample:                       │
│      Sample size required: 248                    │
│      Cost of survey: $2992                        │
│                                                   │
│            Press any key to continue              │
│                                                   │
└─────────────────────────────────────────────────┘
```

If you selected C or D, the program reminds you of what sample size and confidence level you specified and then gives you the cost of the survey. It then gives you an estimate of what the standard deviation and confidence interval would be, assuming a proportionate stratified sample and a simple random sample (Screen 8).

Screen 8

```
┌─────────────────────────────────────────────────────────────┐
│          Stratified Sample Impact Analysis                    │
│          Sample size specified: 500                           │
│          Confidence level specified: 95%                      │
│          Cost of survey: $4000                                │
│                                                               │
│      Assuming a Stratified sample:                            │
│          Standard deviation of proportion estimate...... = .0158 │
│          Confidence interval = ±.0311                         │
│                                                               │
│      Assuming a Random sample:                                │
│          Standard deviation of proportion estimate...... = .0179 │
│          Confidence interval = ±.0352                         │
│                                                               │
│              Press any key to continue.                       │
└─────────────────────────────────────────────────────────────┘
```

At this point, you can press the print screen (PrtSc) key to obtain a hard copy of the results. If you press any other key, you will come to the last menu which allows you to go back and determine the sensitivity of your results to the desired accuracy (A) or desired sample size (B) without having to enter new strata data. Or, you can go back and start again with new strata data (C)(Screen 9).

Screen 9

> Stratified Sample Impact Analysis Select A,B,C, or D
>
> Do you wish to:
>
> A. Use the same strata data to test the effect of confidence interval size on the survey's required sample size.
>
> B. Use the same strata data to test the effect of sample size on the confidence interval.
>
> C. Start again with new strata data.
>
> D. Quit the program.

If you start again, the values you used last time will be the default values this time. If you want to enter new values, simply type in the appropriate numbers.

5.2.4 Assignment Question

A national food manufacturer needed to estimate sales of its brand of creamed corn in grocery stores across the country. Research had been conducted in the past by a national survey firm but the management wished to conduct their own study. It had been found that weekly sales varied substantially by store size and region of the country. The firm had a data base representing the, approximately, 80,000 grocery stores in the nation which it could use as a sampling frame. Included on the list was an estimate of each store's total sales and a code indicating in what region the store was located. Using the data base, the list could be sorted into store size and region and a random sample of stores selected. Once a store was selected, it would cost an average of $20.00 to collect the weekly sales figures for the brand. The fixed cost of selecting the sample and analyzing the results was $2,000.

Management needed to estimate the average sales to an accuracy of $\pm.25$ cases at the 90 percent confidence level. It was suggested that stratification by store size or region of country might reduce the sample size required. It was also suggested that both criteria be used to stratify the sample. This latter approach would result in 15 stratum (3 store sizes × 5 regions).

1. Determine the sample sizes required to achieve the desired accuracy first using the two stratification criteria separately and then in combination.

2. What characteristics of the three sets of criteria lead to the differences in improved efficiency?

3. It was decided that the most the firm could spend on the survey was $18,000, meaning a maximum sample size of 800. What accuracy would be achieved with a sample size of 800?

Weekly Sales of Creamed Corn
(cases)

Region		Small (47%)	Medium (14%)	Large (39%)	All Stores
			Store	Size	
New England and Mid-Atlantic States (21%)	Mean	1.42	17.62	30.10	14.87
	St. Dev.	0.43	5.71	8.27	14.42
East North Central and East South Central States(24%)	Mean	1.37	12.09	26.18	12.55
	St. Dev.	0.57	3.62	5.33	12.32
West North Central and West South Central States(19%)	Mean	0.73	8.61	13.74	6.91
	St. Dev.	0.26	1.55	3.61	6.21
South Atlantic States (17%)	Mean	0.24	3.14	5.21	2.58
	St. Dev.	0.09	1.32	1.80	2.29
Mountain and Mainland Pacific States (19%)	Mean	0.86	7.43	15.30	7.86
	St. Dev.	0.38	2.07	4.74	7.05
All Regions	Mean	0.97	10.18	19.11	9.35
	St. Dev.	0.41	3.84	10.57	10.77

Chapter 6

APPLIED SAMPLING

6.1   Eastern Food Distributors

6.1.1   The Situation

Martha Jones is a marketing researcher working for Do-All, a Toronto-based consulting company. Her company has been asked by Eastern Food Distributors of Halifax to conduct a survey to determine the likelihood that a new restaurant would be profitable if opened up in the Halifax area within a year.

Halifax is a city of approximately 300,000 people, located on the east coast of Canada. It is the business center of eastern Canada; most of the Canadian banks have their eastern headquarters in the city. It is also a government city, being the capital of the province of Nova Scotia and the location of a major naval base. Approximately 250,000 business and government employees visit Halifax each year, 95 percent of them arriving at the city's airport.

Nova Scotia is known as Canada's Ocean Playground and each summer Halifax attracts about 400,000 tourists from central Canada and the New England states. Most of these tourists arrive by car, either taking a ferry to the southern tip of Nova Scotia or driving along the Trans-Canada Highway.

Presently there are about 15 top quality, reasonably expensive (entrées in the $15 to $30 range) restaurants in Halifax similar to the one being considered by Eastern. Most of the major ethnic food types are represented except Indian and Mexican. Seven of the restaurants started business within the last two years, while three have gone out of business in the same time period. It is generally agreed that the demand for good quality restaurants in Halifax is increasing, but the restaurant business has been unsuccessful in predicting the tastes of Halifax restaurant patrons.

Part of the problem is that tastes have been changing over the past few years and what might have been successful five years ago could be a flop today. Sam Davison, the marketing manager for Eastern Food Distributors, wished to avoid the same mistakes so he hired Martha's consulting firm to determine the best strategy for a new restaurant. His questions included the kind of food on the menu, the price range, the atmosphere, the amount of advertising they should do and the feasibility of a location Sam already had in mind. Sam then wanted an estimate of sales.

Martha and Sam agreed to the following alternatives for the food on the menu: Greek, Italian, Indian, North American steak, North American fish, French, and Mexican. As a rough estimate, they felt the restaurant would need to have a sales potential of $750,000 to be feasible. Sam emphasized the need to have the information by March 1st, which left only 15 weeks to design the survey, print the questionnaires, select a sample, conduct the survey, do the analysis and produce a report. He also felt he could not afford to spend more than $12,000 on the survey.

Based on these discussions, Martha developed a a proposal which is summarized in Exhibit 6.1.

Exhibit 6.1
A Summary of the Do-All Proposal

Survey Design

A completed sample of 300 Halifax people is required to estimate preferences in food and atmosphere and to accurately measure the willingness of people to travel to the proposed location.

It is felt that the most cost-efficient method of administering the questionnaire is by mail. Industry standards indicate a 10 percent – 20 percent response rate is average and acceptable for mail-out surveys. We will be enclosing a return envelope and the questionnaire is short and interesting. We therefore feel a 20 percent response rate is likely and acceptable.

We will be picking 1,500 names from the Halifax and surrounding area phone book and using the addresses to mail the questionnaire in January of next year. The selection of 1,500 names from the total Halifax area will ensure that the sample is random and representative.

Timing

	Weeks
Proposal development and meetings with Eastern management	1
Printing of the questionnaires and selection of sample	1
Data collection and coding of responses for computer analysis	4
Analysis of the data	2
Production of the report and presentation of results to Eastern management	2
Total weeks	10

The proposal appeared to be a professional, well-written document and Sam had confidence in the reputation of the firm. The estimated cost of $10,000 was within budget so he gave Martha the go-ahead. Everything went smoothly and, in late February, Sam received his report (Exhibit 6.2).

Exhibit 6.2
Selected Results
of the Do-All Survey

Sampling Results

433 questionnaires were completed and returned (29 percent response rate).

Exhibit 6.2 continued

Selected Results of the Analysis

The preference on a one–ten scale for each type of restaurant is as follows:

Greek.	4.71
Italian	6.68
Indian	4.45
North American steak.	7.10
North American fish.	7.05
French	7.05
Mexican	4.53

The Halifax residents' usage pattern at the 15 restaurants was as follows:

Average spent on lunches last year.	$6.47
Average spent on dinners last year.	$12.30
Average number of visits in last year	3.87

Location

The sales could be improved by locating the restaurant in the suburbs. Many of the potential patrons do not like the idea of driving all the way into the city and were not sure they would find a parking place when they got there.

Price

Most of the potential patrons said they would only go to a restaurant in the price ranges mentioned two or three times per year. However, if the price were reduced, they would probably go considerably more often.

Atmosphere

Respondents were not specific about the kind of atmosphere they felt was appropriate, only that it should be luxurious if the restaurant was going to be priced in the suggested price range.

Exhibit 6.2 continued

Conclusions

1. Higher sales could be achieved by locating the restaurant in the suburbs, offering a North American steak menu and a "luxurious" atmosphere.

2. Luncheon meals for about $7.00 and dinner meals of about $14.00 would appeal to most of the people.

3. The response rate was higher than expected. The higher sample size reduced the chances of bias in the survey.

Sam felt the price of $10,000 for the survey was not unreasonable, although he estimated that less than $2,000 of it was actually spent on collection of the data. The rest covered the consultant's time to develop the design, administer the survey, analyze the data and produce the report.

Unfortunately, he was skeptical about the results. First of all, according to the survey, the greatest preference for a new restaurant was for the most common type of restaurant already in Halifax. In the past few years, the North American steak restaurants had performed worse than all other types. Second, he knew the average bill per person for lunches and dinners reported in the study was 50 percent – 80 percent below the actual average last year. If anything he, would have expected the estimates to be high as people exaggerated the amount they would spend on a meal. Third, most of the heavy users of the more expensive restaurants lived in or near the downtown area, or were staying at one of the downtown hotels, so why did the report recommend a location in the suburbs? And finally, a "luxurious" atmosphere meant nothing to him. All the restaurants in the price range being considered could be said to have "luxurious" interiors.

It has been said that the most valuable kind of research is research that discovers the unexpected. The results of this survey were unexpected, but Sam had the uncomfortable feeling that this research was not the valuable kind.

6.1.2   The Effect of Sampling Decisions on Survey Results

There are five parts in the simulation. The first three parts deal with the mail survey in Halifax and the last two deal with sampling from other lists so that the survey represents more of the population. A quick read of Section 6.2, How to Run Eastern Food Distributors, is recommended before you start playing with the simulation. When you stop making changes to the simulation parameters in one section, you should read the notes for the next section simulation and then continue.

Increasing the Rate of Return

Why is 29 percent an acceptable rate of return? Could Martha have done anything to improve her rate of return?

A decade or more ago, firms would send out boring questionnaires of general interest to the general population. It was not uncommon for a firm to send out 5,000 questionnaires and receive 250 back. But the people who responded were very different from the rest of the population. They filled out questionnaires because they were more insecure, patriotic or bored with life than others.

The survey data was often far more misleading than useful. In some cases, those who responded were no different in their opinions and characteristics than those who didn't respond. However, the researcher could never be sure if this was true or not. So for most cases, the rate of return (percentage of population responding to population reached) had to be improved so that those who responded would not be too different from the population as a whole. That is, the respondents would be representative of the population being studied and there would not be too much bias due to nonresponse.

If there is a chance of significant nonresponse bias, it is important to make sure a significant proportion of those who should respond actually do so. The market researcher has a wide range of incentives/inducements which can be used to increase the rate of response. However, these inducements also cost money, and the market researcher will try to increase the rate of return at a minimum cost per completed questionnaire. Carefully examine the list of incentives/inducements below, their associated costs, and estimated impact on the rate of return (Exhibit 6.3).

Exhibit 6.3
The Cost and Impact of
Incentives and Inducements

	Cost	Additional Response if Incentive Is offered
1. Charitable donation of $1.00: if the questionnaire is returned, the research firm promises to donate $1.00 to charity.	$1.25 per returned questionnaire	+20%
2. Charitable donation of $5.00 for each questionnaire returned.	$4.25 per returned questionnaire	+35%
3. Cash incentive of $1.00: one-dollar bill is enclosed with the questionnaire as thanks in advance for the respondent's cooperation.	$1.00 per household sampled	+30%
4. Cash incentive of $5.00: five-dollar bill is enclosed with the questionnaire.	$5.00 per household sampled	+55%

Exhibit 6.3 continued

	Cost	Additional Response if Incentive Is offered
5. Warning Post Card: the potential respondents are mailed a post card warning that a questionnaire would arrive and seeking their cooperation.	$.50 per household	+20%
6. Reminder post card: those not responding to the first questionnaire are sent a post card reminding them to fill out the questionnaire.	$.50 per questionnaire not returned after first mail out	+30%
7. Pre-mail telephone call: potential respondents are called and informed that a questionnaire will be arriving and their cooperation is sought.	$2.00 per household sampled	+30%
8. Post-mail telephone call: those not responding to the first mail out are called and their cooperation sought.	$2.00 per questionnaire not returned after first mail out	+45%

Exhibit 6.3 continued

	Cost	Additional Response if Incentive Is offered
9. Formatting of questionnaire: the questionnaire is sent to a typesetter to make a formatted, attractive, professional-looking questionnaire.	$500.00 for each survey questionnaire designed	+15%
10. A second questionnaire: Two weeks after the first questionnaire is sent out, a second one is sent to those who have not responded.	$1.00 per questionnaire not returned after first mail out	Depends on number of questionnaires returned after first mailing.
11. Third questionnaire.	$1.00 per questionnaire not returned after first and second mail out	Depends on number of questionnaires returned after first and second mailings.
12. Fourth questionnaire.	$1.00 per questionnaire not returned after first three mail outs	Depends on number of questionnaires already returned.

You should also consider the amount of time you have available to do the survey. When choosing incentives and inducements, estimate their impact on the total time of the survey before including them in your sample design.

Now insert the program disk and do section A of the simulation. This involves the selection of an appropriate combination of incentives to increase the response rate. Do not go on to the next section of the simulation until you have completed this section. Once you have achieved a response rate and cost that you feel is appropriate, print out the results. Be prepared to defend your choice of incentives to the class.

Specifying the Respondent Selection Criteria

Who probably answered the questionnaire? Who should have answered the questionnaire? This section will examine the impact of the first question and illustrate the importance of the second.

A list of those who were more likely to answer the questionnaire might include:

1. the member of the household who is at home when the questionnaire arrives.

2. the person who has more time.

3. the person who enjoys filling out questionnaires.

4. the person who feels a commitment to fill out questionnaires.

5. the person who goes to restaurants more often.

    The demographics Martha collected indicated the following.

    - 70 percent of the respondents were females.
    - 65 percent had incomes below the city's median income as reported by Statistics Canada.
    - The median number of visits to the restaurants studied was 2 per year.
    - 30 percent were unemployed.
    - 60 percent had blue-collar jobs.

It appears that Martha did not define a sample population; if she did, she did nothing to ensure that the correct person responded to the questionnaire. The statistics above indicate that she didn't get a random sample of adults, if that was her aim. Perhaps a random sample of adults is not the correct sample unit for this study anyway. Is it reasonable to expect all adults to answer questions about the 15 most expensive restaurants in the city?

Before you proceed to section B, carefully define the sample population and decide what respondent selection criteria you would have used in this study. Some respondent selection options are presented in section B of the program. Try these options, select the criteria you feel are best, and print out the results of the survey for discussion in class.

You will notice a drastic drop in the response rate when you select some of the criteria. This is because a large proportion of those you sent questionnaires to no longer fit your criteria, and they have simply thrown out the questionnaire. For example, a response rate of 32 percent may be a result of the fact that 60 percent of the those you sent the questionnaire to did not meet your criteria. Your actual response rate was 80 percent (32 percent of 40 percent). Unless you asked everybody to mail back a questionnaire or card, there is no way of knowing for sure the true response rate.

Handling Nonresponse Bias

Increasing the response rate from 40 percent to 80 percent in order to reduce the possibility of response bias can be very expensive. It may be more economical to simply estimate the amount of bias due to nonresponse and take that into account when you do your analysis. If there is no bias, then you won't have wasted money trying to increase the rate of return. You might instead spend it on increasing the sample size, thereby reducing sampling error in order to reduce total error.

One method of estimating nonresponse bias is to examine the average responses of those who responded to the first mailing, the second mailing, the third mailing, and so on. You then look for a trend in the averages which would indicate nonrespondents are different from respondents. This can be done in the simulation by first sending out one questionnaire, then two, then three, printing out the results each time, and calculating the average of those who responded to each successive mailing of questionnaires. If there is an obvious trend in the results, you can estimate the average response of those who have not yet responded and derive the average for the whole population.

Another method of estimating nonresponse bias is to conduct a survey of a small sample of nonrespondents. This survey is usually conducted by telephone so that results are quickly available. A considerable effort is made to achieve a high rate of return since it is those who are least likely to respond to any survey that must be reached in a survey of nonrespondents. Up to seven or eight calls may be made to reach those selected for the follow-up survey. This is, of course, very costly and potentially time consuming which is why only 50 or so nonrespondents are selected. An estimate can be derived for the population once the averages for the nonrespondents and responders are known, as well as their relative proportions in the population.

Of course, analysis for non-response bias is only necessary if your response rate is so low that it makes the potential impact of this bias significant. A third option, therefore, is to offer enough incentives/inducements so that a reasonable response rate is achieved. You can then ignore the problem. This has the added advantage of allowing you to conduct your analysis without having to be concerned that your results are simply a result of non-response bias.

Section C of the simulation gives you the opportunity to conduct a telephone survey of up to 50 nonrespondents. You might wish to go back and change your incentives and the number of mailings of questionnaires sent out before you do the survey so that you will keep within budget. When deciding to use this method of handling nonresponse bias, consider the amount of time required to do the survey and to incorporate the results in your analysis, as well as the cost. You will have the same options for handling nonresponse bias if you do a mail survey of tourists in section E of the simulation.

Selection of Sampling Lists

By using the telephone book for addresses, Martha left out several important groups of people:

1. Unlisted: 10 percent of Halifax households who don't want their telephone number listed in the book.

2. Nonlisted: 10 percent of Halifax households who have just moved in to the area in the last year and have a new telephone number.

3. Visiting business and government employees.

4. Tourists.

What percentage of all dollars spent at the kind of restaurant being considered do you think these groups represent?

	% of Halifax Households	% of Expenditure at These Restaurants
Unlisted	10%	_____
Nonlisted	10%	_____
Visiting Business and Government Officials	0%	_____
Tourists	0%	_____
Customers with numbers listed in the telephone book	80%	_____

How do you feel these groups will differ in taste from restaurant goers interviewed in Martha's survey? Not measuring the opinions of these people will introduce bias into the survey results. However, measuring their opinions will add to the cost of the survey and you have to decide whether to include them or not.

Two new lists are provided for you to sample in section D of the simulation. Visiting business and government employees can be reached at the Halifax airport. The airport administration has agreed to let you survey people in the lounge as they are waiting to board their airplane. The interviewer first asks a qualifying question to identify visiting business and government employees and then administers the questionnaire.

It will cost you $350.00 in training costs if you do any interviewing at the airport, an average of $.50 for each business and government employee approached, another $4.00 for every completed interview. There would be an added cost of $5.00 for every completed interview if you offer a free watch pen as an incentive. The added time to design the questionnaire, train the interviewers, do the extra analysis and incorporate the results into the report will add two weeks to the study and $2,000 in consulting fees.

Surveying Tourists

Tourists can also be surveyed at the airport, but only 5% of tourists come by air and very few come in January. However, as an enterprising consultant, you have managed to obtain access to the registration book for the Citadel Inn, one of the larger hotels in the downtown area. There are some short-comings of this source as a sample list for tourists visiting Halifax. However, given the time constraints, it is the best you can come up with. If you decide to use it for a mail survey, your added consulting fees will be $2,000.

You will also have the option of conducting a telephone survey of up to 50 nonrespondents, so keep this in mind when you choose your incentives and number of questionnaire mailings. The consulting time required will add one week to the survey and $1,500 in consultant fees. If you decide to send more waves of questionnaires or anything else that adds time to the length of the study that you didn't do in the Halifax survey, you will have to increase your estimate of the total time required for the study accordingly.

Summary

Having examined the effect of all these decisions individually, you should carefully consider the options and make the decisions that Martha did not. Be sure to record or print out the results of your survey for comparison with others. When deciding on the options, consider the cost and time ramifications and weigh these against the benefits. Go with the survey design you feel will meet the needs of the client while being "reasonably" priced.

One last thought: perhaps the time and cost constraints specified by Sam were unreasonable. If so, do you get him to change the specifications, refuse to do the survey, or do a survey that is not as "correct" as it should be?

6.1.3 Case Assignment

1. What inducements/incentives would you use for the Halifax mail survey?

2. How could the lack of respondent selection criteria in the original sample design affect the results? What respondent selection criteria would you select in section B? Why these criteria?

3. Would you do either a follow-up survey of nonrespondents to the Halifax mail survey or a trend analysis of responses to the waves of questionnaires sent out? Why or why not?

4. How would you incorporate the results of this analysis of nonresponse bias into your estimates of means?

5. Given the sampling element you defined, what are the sampling units for the Halifax mail survey?

6. What was your response rate for the Halifax mail survey? Is it a reasonable response rate? Why? How would the use of respondent selection criteria affect the calculation of response rates? What could have been done in order to calculate a correct response rate if criteria other than a random sample of adults was used?

7. What were the results of your mail survey of Halifax households? What are your conclusions?

8. Would you survey business and government employees at the airport? How do they fit into your defined sample population?

9. Would you use an incentive (the watch pen)?

10. What would be your actual sampling list for the airport survey?

11. Are the preferences of the visiting business and government employees different from the preferences of Halifax residents? If so, are these differences in the direction you would hypothesize them to be?

12. Would you survey tourists? How do they fit into your defined population?

13. Are incentives for the tourists to respond to the survey more or less important than incentives for the Halifax residents? What incentives did you use and why?

14. Are the tourist's preferences different from the preferences of the other two groups?

15. What respondent selection criteria would be appropriate for this survey?

16. How appropriate was the use of the hotel's guest list as a sample list? What biases would be introduced? What would you do instead?

17. How would you estimate bias due to nonresponse? What were the results of your analysis?

18. How much would your survey have cost? Be sure to include the costs of designing, analyzing and reporting the results for each of the steps in the survey you do. Is this a reasonable amount?

19. Using the results of your survey, what do you think would be the most successful type of new restaurant in Halifax next year (all else equal)?

20. Error in estimates come from two main sources, sampling error (a function of sample size) and bias. Bias in responses can be caused by many things. One common source of bias is caused by asking the wrong people the questions so that certain elements in the population are under- or over- represented. How much of the total error in the original study conducted by Martha was sampling error and how much was bias due to the final sample not representing the population correctly? (State your estimates in percentage terms, a very rough estimate is all that is required.) How effective would increasing the sample size have been in reducing total error? What is the relative impact of proper sample design on total error (correct selection of respondent in the household, surveying groups not represented in the original survey, and reducing nonresponse or deriving estimates of nonresponse bias)? Was it worth the extra cost to improve the sample design?

6.2   How to Run Eastern Food Distributors

The program is designed to allow you to address each of the major issues in the case sequentially. You should, therefore, start with section A, Selection of Incentives and Number of Mailings, by typing *a* and pressing the enter sign (Screen 1). You may not finish the case in one session. To start again, you should start at section A and re-enter your selected values and assumptions, as later sections may use these values in the calculations.

Screen 1

Eastern Food Distributors Limited

     A. Selection of Incentives and Number of Mailings
     B. Selection of Respondent Selection Criteria
     C. Handling Non-Response Bias from the Halifax
        Residential Mail Survey
     D. Visiting Government and Business Employees Survey
     E. Tourists Survey
     Q. Quit

        Please select A-E, or Q to quit:

6.2.1   Selection of Incentives and Number of Mailings

Press *N* or *Y* to indicate whether you wish to select a particular incentive (Screen 2). When it is impossible to do two actions (that is, send out both $1.00 as an incentive and, $5.00 as an incentive) the program will only allow you to choose one of the actions. See the case for a detailed discussion of the meaning and possible impact of each alternative. Once you have made your choice (or at any other time), you can move to a particular action using the up and down arrows located on the number keypad. When you have decided on the incentives you will use, and how many times the questionnaires will be mailed, hit the page down (PgDn) key which is also located on the numeric keypad.

Screen 2

```
              ┌─────────────────────────────────┐
              │ Eastern Food Distributors Limited │
              └─────────────────────────────────┘
                   SURVEY INCENTIVE SELECTION

      Cash donation of $1.00 .............................. N
      Cash donation of $5.00 .............................. N

      Cash incentive of $1.00 ............................. N
      Cash incentive of $5.00 ............................. N

      Send warning post card .............................. N
      Send reminder post card ............................. N

      Pre-mailing telephone call .......................... N
      Post-mailing telephone call ......................... N

      Formatting of questionnaire ......................... Y

      Send a 2nd questionnaire ............................ Y
      Send a 3rd questionnaire ............................ N
      Send a 4th questionnaire ............................ N

        Use ↑↓ to move around, Press PgDn when done.
```

You will then be asked to enter the number of households to which you wish to send questionnaires. Hitting the carriage return will accept the value already in the box. You can enter any integer value from 1 to 999999. If you make a mistake when entering the number, you can use the delete key located above the carriage return to erase the numbers, or you can hit the left arrow and enter the complete value. Hit the carriage return when you are finished.

The computer will then do the survey and present the results to you (Screen 3). If you want a hard copy of these results, press *Y*. The print out will indicate what incentives you used, how many mailings and the results of your survey. If there is trouble printing, the computer will ask you to fix the problem or hit any key to abort the printing process. If you get this message, check for the following possible problems. Correcting the problem should produce a printout.

1. You have no printer (then hit any key).

2. The cable is disconnected or, if more than one computer uses a printer, the computer selector switch is turned to another computer.

3. The printer is turned off.

4. The printer is not "on line."

5. The printer is out of paper.

6. The printer cover is not closed.

Screen 3

| | Eastern Food Distributors Limited |
Based on response on a ten-point scale the preference for a new restaurant of each type is as follows.

	Mean	Variance
Greek	4.29	7.33
Italian	6.25	3.35
Indian	3.92	5.16
N.A. steak	5.92	5.08
N.A fish	6.46	3.67
French	6.71	7.08
Mexican	4.02	3.72
Lunch (Avg. $ spent)	6.19	4.44
Dinner (Avg. $ spent)	10.83	12.25
# visits in last year	3.23	4.57

Number of questionnaires mailed 1000
The response rate was 68.7%
Number of completed questionnaires 687
Total cost = $ 2986.37
Cost per completed questionnaire $ 4.34

Print out the results (Y/N) ?

6.2.2 Selection of Respondent Selection Criteria

You will first be asked to select the incentives and number of mailings (Screen 4). Simply hitting the PgDn key selects the options you specified in section A. You will then be asked to select your respondent selection criteria. The first selection is to conduct a random sample of adults. If you do this, you will not be asked to specify any further criteria.

If you do not select a random sample of adults, you will first be given the option of selecting any person in the household who is over 19 years of age. You can also specify that the respondent must have visited a restaurant two or more times in the last year or six or more times in the last year. If you select neither of these criteria, then it is assumed the respondents in the household will decide whether they have had sufficient experience to answer the questions.

You can then specify whether you wish to survey males only or females only. If you specify neither, it is assumed that either could respond as long as they meet the other selection criteria.

Screen 4

```
┌─────────────────────────────────────────────────────────────────┐
│                                                                   │
│              ┌─────────────────────────────────────┐             │
│              │ Eastern Food Distributors Limited │             │
│              └─────────────────────────────────────┘             │
│                                                                   │
│         Respondent must be over 19 (Y/N): │ Y │                 │
│                                                                   │
│         Respondent must have visited a restaurant                 │
│         two or more times in the last year (Y/N): │ Y │         │
│                                                                   │
│         Respondent must have visited restaurants                  │
│         more than six times in the last year (Y/N): │ N │       │
│                                                                   │
│         Males only (Y/N): │ N │                                 │
│         Females only (Y/N): │ N │                               │
│                                                                   │
│                                                                   │
│         Use ↑↓ to move around, Press PgDn when done.              │
│                                                                   │
└─────────────────────────────────────────────────────────────────┘
```

After selecting the number of households to be mailed questionnaires, you will again receive the results of the survey. If you request a hard copy of the results, the printout will now specify your selection criteria.

6.2.3   Survey of Nonrespondents

Selection of this option will automatically produce the results of the survey as there are no other decisions that need to be made. It is assumed you will conduct a telephone survey with at least six attempts to reach the respondents and you will aim for a completed sample size of 50.

Since you are calling the households, you will be able to identify those households that do not qualify as elements in your population and they are excluded from your response rate calculations. The number of nonqualifying households identified is reported on the screen.

6.2.4   Visiting Business and Government Employees

Again, the design is largely predetermined. You will only have to decide upon the sample size (the number of qualified respondents approached) and whether to offer an incentive for respondent participation.

6.2.5   Survey of Tourists

In this section, you will first be asked to enter the number of households to be mailed questionnaires. You can then select the incentives you will use in the survey, just as you did for the Halifax survey. You do not have to choose respondent selection criteria for this survey.

Again, as was the case for the Halifax survey, you will have the opportunity to conduct a telephone survey of nonrespondents.

Chapter 7

QUESTIONNAIRE DESIGN

7.1 OMNIBUS POLLS

Omnibus Polls Inc. was located in a major Great Lakes port city. It grew out of the Urban Issues Research Center of the city's University. The center had been almost entirely dependent upon federal grants and research contracts which had nearly dried up with the change in administrations. The center director's personal history of support for liberal causes put it on something less than an equal footing in competing for the remaining federal monies.

The center had a reputation for nearly faultless study design, sample selection and interviewing. The director, Lars Svenson, and chief statistician, Franz Pearson, were given much of the credit for its high quality work. When the university withdrew its remaining support, they decided to start a private research firm and founded Omnibus Polls.

Omnibus did not compete for the quick and dirty sort of contracts that were the bread and butter of many similar-sized firms. If someone wanted a study consisting of 50 street corner intercepts, Omnibus's researchers would suggest one of a number of firms that specialized in that sort of work, even if the request came from an established Omnibus client. In order to build upon and reinforce the now defunct center's reputation for quality, Omnibus would only conduct studies done "by the book."

7.1.1 The Omnibus Poll

The principal product was the Omnibus Poll itself. Conceived by Lars, the Omnibus Poll consisted of three parts and was both a gold mine and a tremendously successful promotional device. The core instrument consisted of a number of questions designed to monitor attitudes towards a set of social trends of concern to major corporate clients. The results were reported and interpreted in *Omnibus Says* which was distributed only to a select set of subscribers. The subscription charge was never publicly revealed and was believed to be negotiated with individual subscribers on a "whatever the market will bear" basis. Pearson had been heard to boast that subscription revenue covered all overhead expenses including salaries for himself and Lars. (Both lived very well.)

Part 2 of the poll was carefully designed to generate publicity for the firm itself, by collecting data that could be used as the basis for high visibility press releases. Once a week the principals sat down and scanned the headlines of national, regional and local newspapers to identify issues that were "hot." These issues suggested the questions for this section. The only selection criterion here was that the finding of a reputable polling organization on the subject would receive substantial media attention. Since Omnibus's primary customers were corporations and major corporate divisions head-quartered in the city, emotional or humorous local issues were ideal. Recent topics included a scandal in the city ambulance service and the proposal to diaper the mounted-police horses.

Pearson had developed this promotional device and its success exceeded his fondest expectations. An Omnibus press release was almost never ignored and was usually used without major modifications. The producers of the most popular drive-time radio shows regularly called Lars to see if he, Franz, or an Omnibus Associate (the title outside consultants agreed to use in interviews) had anything new that would provide material for a feature. Of course, they always did. News from Omnibus had almost become a regular item. This was extremely valuable publicity because a very large proportion of the executive population listened to these shows. It was obtained at little cost other than adding a question or two to interviews that were going to be conducted anyway.

The third portion of the Omnibus Poll was for sale, in whole or in part. This section was contracted on an a la carte basis; a client could pay for the insertion of a single question or buy this entire part of the study. This was viewed as a client development vehicle. Inserting a question or two allowed a firm to sample Omnibus's services without a major resource commitment. As they came to rely more heavily on Omnibus, they were encouraged to move from the Omnibus Poll to independent studies focusing entirely on their own research problems. Results here were entirely private and proprietary and were reported only to the client at whose behest an item had been added.

Omnibus was a bare bones operation. Svenson, Pearson, a secretary-receptionist, and two research assistants were the only full-time employees. Though they could be used somewhat interchangeably, one research assistant specialized in drafting and precoding questionnaires and the other in entering data into the university computer on which Omnibus had a contract account. Interviewing was done by a relatively stable cadre of part-time interviewers, mostly housewives and university students.

The normal flow for part 3 of an Omnibus Poll questionnaire was from Alvin, the research assistant who drafted it, to Lars or Franz for initial editing. Most of the time the draft then went to an outside consultant, usually someone at the university who had experience in the area(s) being investigated, for comment, and suggestions.

Alvin left rather suddenly to follow his steady to a houseboat commune near Sausalito on San Francisco Bay. Elaine, his replacement, has just presented the results of her first attempt at questionnaire writing (Exhibit 7.2) to Lars. The sponsors included a) the campaign committee for a candidate in the upcoming municipal election and b) an entrepreneur interested in converting old-style neighborhood groceries to convenience stores not affiliated with the major convenience store chains. In addition, Elaine had been instructed to draft replacements for a few demographic items as part of a continuing process of item testing and improvement.

Lars had agreed to address the university's market research class. Whenever he did one of these "gigs" he liked to take along a real-world problem to add pizazz to his presentation. Since he had just received the draft, he decided to kill two birds with one stone and have the class (yours) make comments and suggestions. By the end of the hour he could have his service to the university done, and the questionnaire cleaned up. With a little luck the class would even provide some fresh insights. Lars prepared a handout (Exhibit 7.1) to assist in his presentation.

Exhibit 7.1
Preparing Questionnaires

Writing Questions

There is no single right way to ask a question. To begin with, one should assure oneself that respondents a) can be expected to have the information, b) will be able to recall the information, and c) can and will answer the question accurately. Further respondent time and effort are valuable commodities. Make sure that a piece of information bears upon your research problem or that a variable has a place in your analysis plan before you ask a question. All too frequently an item is included because someone thinks it is commonly asked rather than in the belief that it has a bearing on the issue at hand.

Don't waste time with "do good and avoid evil" items on which only one response is possible or likely. "Did you consider price when you bought. . ." would almost surely be answered in the affirmative, if only because most are conditioned to the view that they ought to have considered price even if they didn't do so. Exceptions here would be rhetorical questions designed to build interest or rapport and questions asked of a prescreened sample to insure that those interviewed did, in fact, meet the selection criteria.

Common Problems

Unclear Words

Words used must have a single meaning which is common across respondents. This is not as easy as it sounds. For example, one might ask respondents how many sodas they consume in an average week. Some would reply with an estimate of total soft drink consumption. Others, even heavy consumers of soft drinks, might indicate none at all, reserving "soda" for carbonated or seltzer water or an ice cream confection.

Be careful of weasel words such as *regularly* or *frequently*. These can have entirely different meanings to different respondents. "Do you regularly serve wine with meals?" An affirmative response might mean anything from twice a day to most holidays.

One must consider the knowledge, background, and verbal skills of respondents. A medical doctor might respond readily and accurately if asked if he had had pertussis. Most persons would be more comfortable with "Have you had whooping cough?"

Biased Wording

Biased questions contain clues causing respondents to reply in one way or the other, regardless of their true position on the subject. Most people tend to be agreeable and to "side with the angels." Any indication of the interviewer's or the sponsor's position ("Don't you agree that. . .") would produce an inordinate number of conforming responses.

A question may be biased in many subtle ways such as:

- indicating that one response is the correct response;

- associating some position with a prestigious individual or organization;

- using value-laden words to describe a position, attitude or object.

Leading Questions

This category of error is very close to biased words in that it refers to providing cues in the question that lead the respondent to a particular answer. Naming a brand or company may produce more favorable responses towards that brand or company. Asking respondents if they own a Sunbeam mixer would probably produce a greater apparent incidence of Sunbeam ownership than if they were simply asked to name the brand of mixer they own. It would probably also inflate subsequent ratings of mixers and particularly Sunbeam mixers.

Respondents would probably assume Sunbeam, or at least an appliance maker, was the sponsor of the study. There is a tendency to be supportive of study sponsors and their products.

Implicit Alternatives

The relevant alternatives to a question should be clearly stated. The following questions would probably produce quite different responses.

1. "Would you take a promotion that required working on Sunday?"

2. "Would you take a promotion that required working on Sunday if turning it down meant losing your job?"

The largest problem with not making alternatives explicit is that question writing is left to the imagination of the respondent. The researcher does not know exactly what question the respondent is answering.

The researcher may consider only one alternative to be reasonable or relevant. However, every respondent may see the situation differently. Instead of having a hundred subjects responding to a single question, the researcher may end up with a hundred questions, each with an n of 1. (See Implied Assumption and Frame of Reference.)

Implied Assumption

The answer to a question may depend upon one or more implicit assumptions. Consider "Are you in favor of mandatory nutritional labeling on food products?" Implicit are the assumptions that a) consumers will employ this information in choosing foods, b) use of the information will result in improved nutrition, and c) the improvement will be great enough to justify the increased costs and greater intervention by government.

A respondent who did not share a belief in these assumptions as to outcomes, but who believed there would be added costs, would not be supportive. A better question would be "Would you favor mandatory nutritional labeling of food products if it would result in. . .?" It is always best to have all cards on the table.

Even in the improved form, it is necessary that the researcher and respondents have a common understanding of the phrase "mandatory nutritional labeling." (See Unclear Words.)

Frame of Reference

Frame of reference refers to the perspective adopted by the respondent in answering the question. Differences can be induced by subtle changes in the wording of a question.

Consider a) "Are electric utilities making satisfactory progress in dealing with acid rain?" and b) "Are you satisfied with the progress of electric utilities in dealing with acid rain?"

Question (a) seems to call for some sort of an objective appraisal from a societal perspective. Question (b) is much more personal and subjective in tone. Responses to (b) might be much more heavily influenced by whether the respondent was a resident of Maine or a shareholder in an Ohio Valley coal-burning utility.

No single perspective is correct. The research must insure that the one induced is appropriate to the purposes of the study.

Double-barreled Questions

A double-barreled question exists when a single question can be viewed as requiring two different responses; for example, "How do you feel about the sweetness and the alcohol content of the new light wines?" The respondent is asked to rate two stimuli, "sweetness" and "alcohol content." The researcher simply does not know what a response means in such instances.

A favorable response might indicate that the respondent approved of both. Alternatively, through some mental balancing, the respondent may be trading off among excess sweetness and a desire for a lower alcohol content or a desired sweetness level and a sacrifice in alcohol. (Also see Complex Question.) Be particularly wary of any Question containing the conjunction and.

Complex Questions

Here we refer to long and involved questions that are difficult for the respondent to understand. Reserchers also have difficulty interpreting the responses reliably. "Since a woman's right to control her own body is pre-eminent, there should be abortion on demand." A respondent endorsing this position presumably accepts both the premise, the conclusion, and the linkage. However, one could reject it on many grounds unrelated to the abortion issue, such as fathers' rights, or the belief that no single right should stand over others.

One frequently makes this sort of an error while trying to avoid other faults, such as implied assumptions. The media frequently report the outcome of studies by major polling organizations that seem to have employed overly complex questions. One hopes that these have been thoroughly pretested to determine how they would be interpreted by respondents.

Requiring Estimates

This is a special case of asking respondents for information they do not have. They are thus required to make some sort of an estimate or generalization.

Consider the question "How much did you spend for lunches last year?" Few people have this information and an estimate based on general behavior would probably be given.

It would be far better to ask respondents about more recallable facts, such as the frequency of eating the noon meal and the amount spent yesterday or last week. One must, of course, insure that "yesterday or last week" would not be expected to be exceptions to the respondents' normal routine. That is, do not adopt this procedure if data is being collected during the holiday season and you are attempting to estimate normal expenditure levels.

Respondent Unwilling or Unable to Answer

Respondents are likely to be unwilling to answer questions viewed as intimate or highly personal. Further, this sort of question is particularly likely to elicit socially acceptable or conforming responses from those that do answer. Some respondents are influenced more by the way their response will make them appear to the interviewer than by the true state of affairs. If a study includes this sort of topic, one may be well advised to consider something other than direct questioning.

Even if they are willing, respondents may be unable to answer or to answer accurately. There are many possible reasons. Respondents are often unaware of the many factors influencing their behavior. Forgetting occurs. Subsequent experiences with a product may influence the reported importance of evaluative criteria. A respondent may never have heard of some product of issue, yet the fact that they are being questioned implies that they should have.

Given that they are participating, the easiest thing for a respondent to do is to give some answer. It is incumbent upon the researcher to establish that there is a high probability that members of the population studied have the information he desires and will be willing to give it in response to the question in its present form.

7.1.2 Case Assignment

Requirements

The draft questionnaire with which you will be working is shown below (Exhibit 7.2). To save machine time, study it carefully and identify problems you see and corrections you think should be made.

Lars's handout contained a list of pitfalls that the inexperienced question writer may fall into. Study it carefully. This list is also included in the program *Omnibus Polls* and can be called at any time to refresh your memory.

To complete this exercise, select *Omnibus Polls* from the main menu. You will be taken through the questionnaire shown below, one question at a time. For each question you will be asked to identify shortcomings (up to three—how bad can one question be?) that you find with the way in which it is written. A graphic display will then show how much of an improvement correcting the errors you detected might have made.

Rewriting Questions

The questionnaire shown in Exhibit 7.2 is stored on disk 1 as QUEST.TXT This file may be loaded into any wordprocessor to rewrite questions you think need improvement.

Exhibit 7.2
Questionnaire for Analysis

1. Do you favor the mayor's much discussed stand on prayer in the schools?

2. Is enough being done to solve the problem of sewers backing up into basements in the south end?

3. Should stores and restaurants in the city be required to carry sugar-free gum?

4. All things considered, should municipal taxes be reduced?

5. Should the city purchasing department be required to buy from local sources even if it meant paying higher prices or taking lower quality, since that would reduce unemployment?

6. Is the city bus service adequate?

7. Do you feel that there are too many coin-operated newspaper racks in the historic redevelopment area east of West Street?

8. Should the city increase its ownership of the electric company from 49% to 51%?

9. Does councilman Jones spend enough time preparing for meetings of the city council?

10. Do you agree with the Municipal Medical Society that stricter ordinances are needed governing home births?

11. Did you read candidate Enarson's article on the state of the local economy in the *Globe Enquirer* last Sunday?

12. Are the new building code provisions for tornado-proofing high-rise buildings adequate?

13. Did you vote for Mayor Lundstrom or his opponent in last year's landslide election?

14. Do you favor requiring the bus company to serve the major routes until 30 minutes after the bars close?

15. Should the city treasurer be required to maintain a deposit in a local bank equal to anticipated spending for the next 30 days?

16. How much did your family spend on food last year?

17. What proportion of that was spent in neighborhood stores?

18. Are the prices and merchandise assortment in convenience stores adequate?

19. Do convenience stores serve a useful function?

20. Should convenience stores frequented by school children be prevented from selling cigarettes and beer?

21. Aren't all children being unjustly discriminated against when some convenience store owners will only allow three in at a time because of the misbehavior of a few?

22. Don't you believe that neighborhood stores should carry fresh fruits and vegetables?

23. Are the higher prices charged by convenience stores justified?

24. How far would you travel for a substantial reduction in food prices?

25. Don't you feel guilty when you run out of milk and have to buy it at a convenience store?

26. Do you agree with the position of the Consumers' Union that there is inadequate competition in the grocery trade?

27. How many times did you shop at a supermarket last month?

28. Is the service better at owner operated grocery stores?

29. Do you use Farmer Baxter's dairy products?

30. How old are you?

Chapter 8
STAT

8.1   Introduction to STAT

STAT is a set of easy-to-use, yet powerful statistical procedures. It is capable of handling most problems assigned in the marketing research course. In fact, it will handle the vast majority of real-world marketing problems. At any time the STAT main menu is on the screen, you will have the opportunity to review the instructions below.

The authors have done their best to check for and prevent errors that would prove fatal to the course of a run. However, the really inventive user can probably find ways to get bombed out of a subprogram. If this happens to you, you can probably recover by hitting the *Esc* key and carriage return (C/R) or enter. If this does not return you to the STAT main menu, then you will have to start over from the beginning, rebooting the system if necessary.

There is an quicker way to get into STAT than by selecting it from the main menu. You may wish to use it. Simply place Disk 2 in a drive (preferably A) and type *MAIN* and carriage return.

Upon beginning the main program, you will be asked whether you want to a) analyze an existing data set (disk) or b) enter new data via the keyboard. An existing data set may be either one provided by the authors or one created by the user in a previous session.

8.1.1   Creating a Data Set

If you are entering new data, you will be asked how many cases, and variables you have. You must know the number of variables; new variables cannot be added later. If you do not know the number of cases enter the maximum (225). After you have entered all of your data and the computer is asking for the next case's data, type *1e9* and hit return. This signals the computer to go to the next step.

Each variable is automatically identified by a variable number, for example V-1. You will be given the option of identifying them by names of up to ten characters (letters or numbers). It is wise to do so as it makes it much easier to use the data set at a later date.

When you have completed entering your data, you will be given the opportunity to review it and, if necessary, make corrections. This is a good idea since even the best of us can make tpying errrors.

After checking for correctness you will be asked whether or not you want to save your data on disk. It is wise to do so even if you don't think you will ever need the data again. It is better to save a data set and have to delete it later than not to save it and later, wish it were available so you could do some further analyses.

Data may be entered in one or several sittings. In either case you will have the option of making corrections to the values entered. Your data may be saved on disk both before and after making corrections.

It is a good idea to have more than one copy of your data, preferably on separate disks. When adding to or correcting a data file, the following procedure is one the authors find useful.

Have two formatted disks available. Enter the data and save it on disk 1. Make a second copy on disk 2 using the DOS copy command. If you make changes later, write over the file on disk 1 with the changed data. After further additions or changes, write over the file on disk 2. Continue this procedure of alternating disks and you will always have a reasonably current back-up copy of your data. You will not lose a great deal of work if something should go wrong with one of your disk files. Additional copies should be made when all additions and corrections have been completed.

BE PARTICULARLY CAREFUL when deciding whether to add to or write over a file when you are informed that a file already exists with the name you have chosen for the file you want to create. STAT will alert you to the situation. Only you can choose the correct action. There are a few cautions you should keep in mind.

- Do not make corrections to a file and then add it to the end of an existing data file. If you do so, the file will contain the original values followed by the corrected values. It would be difficult to sort this out and it cannot be done within STAT.

- It is a good idea to execute a save after every few cases when entering data. If you do so, you must load the entire file by choosing Option 12 before performing any analysis. This is so that STAT can initialize itself.

- Be extremely careful about writing over any file. You can wipe out a tremendous amount of work in a careless instant.

- If ever you are in doubt, choose a different file name or use a different disk. It is a simple matter to go back and clean house later.

8.1.2   Missing Values

It is the exception, rather than the rule, to have data for all variables for all cases. This is particularly true of questionnaire data; there will almost always be missing values on some variables. When entering your data, you will need to pick some code which is assigned whenever a case does not have a proper value for a variable. The missing value for a variable code must be one which no valid case can ever have. Since this must be selected in advance, it is desirable to assign a value which a variable cannot take on, e.g., one might use 999 or -9 whenever age is missing.

The user is prompted to specify missing values at the beginning of each procedure. There are seldom defaults. A case will be deleted from a procedure if it has missing data on any variable used in that procedure (listwise deletion). For example, assume that you have selected the first eight variables to be available in stepwise regression and that a case has missing data on V-1. That case will be excluded from the analysis, even if V-1 never enters the regression analysis.

8.1.3   Subprograms

The STAT main menu will present the following options.

1. *Descriptive Statistics: Interval Variables*.   Mean, variance, standard deviation, coefficient of variation.

2. *Pearson Correlation*. Finds the Correlation among any two variables.

   Most of the preceding statistics are also output by multiple regression or can be calculated from the values produced.

3. *Simple Regression*. Regresses one independent variable on one dependent variable.

4. *Frequencies*. Determines median and mode, and produces frequency distribution and histogram. Only handles values in the range 1-1,000, but includes recoding option. Detailed instructions are included in the procedure and in section 8.3.

5. *T-tests*. User specifies codes identifying groups on an independent variable and selects the dependent variable. Routine displays the value of t, the degrees of freedom and the significance of t for both the pooled and the separate variance estimates. The F test for equality of variance needed to select the appropriate approach is displayed.

6. *Crosstabulation*. Analyzes relationships among variables displayed in two-way (up to 4-by-4) tables. Runs in two modes. In **Integer** mode, the levels on the variables are designated by integer values supplied by the user. In **Recode** mode, levels are ranges of values which are recoded by the program (e.g., income brackets). Computes and displays Chi Square statistic and degrees of freedom.

   Both procedures 4. *Frequencies* and 6. *Crosstabs* provide a recoding capability. These recodings are only in effect while using that subprogram. Those accomplished with 9. *Data Modification*, remain in effect for the remainder of the statistics run.

7. *Multiple Regression (Stepwise)*. ´This routine goes through a number of steps in developing a final regression model including a dependent variable and up to eight independent variables. In addition to identifying the variables, the user must specify values for F to enter and F to remove. The F ratio indicates the significance of a variable's contribution to the explanatory power of the model.

   To enter on any step, a variable must have an F value greater than F to enter. F values may change as new variables are included. If an F value for a variable already in the model declines below F to remove, it will be taken out. A variable removed on any step will be considered for reentry on later steps.

   You must consult an F table to select an F to enter. For example, you may want all variables entering to be significant at the 0.1 level. If you expect 3 variables to enter and have around 125 cases, you would select an F to enter of 2.13.

8. *ANOVA (Analysis of Variance)*. ANOVA does a one- or two-way (4-by-4 maximum) analysis of variance using the fixed effects model appropriate to the most common marketing applications. The user is required to identify the factor(s), the codes identifying levels on the factors and the dependent variable. Missing values on the factors or the dependent variable may be designated.

9. *Data Modification*. This subprogram may be used to modify the values stored for a variable. It runs in two major modes. **Recode** takes some value or range of values and recodes them to new values. For example, take a marital status variable coded as 1 = single, 2 = married, 3 = divorced, 4 = widowed. You might wish to combine divorced and

widowed because the numbers in each category are small. This could be accomplished by recoding 3 to 4 (or 4 to 3) which would cause the computer to believe there is only one category (4 or 3).

In **Arithmetic** mode, one may perform computations using the values of variables. For example, if you have stored as variables sales in units and unit price, you could multiply the two to determine dollar revenue.

The recode subprogram contains extensive instructions.

10. *Instructions*. The user may return to these instructions any time the STAT main menu is displayed.

11. *Load a File*. Whenever the STAT main menu is displayed, you may load a new file. The file then in memory is lost but disk copies are not affected. One must ALWAYS exercise this option OR leave STAT and begin all over after adding to a data file or building a file a few cases at a time.

12. *List and/or Change Data*. This procedure allows you to examine and, if necessary, change data recorded for individual cases. One might need to do this if it became apparent in the course of a run that some case contained an error. For example, you might find that the mean of a variable with a legitimate range of one to five was 1,000. A large value has obviously been entered for one or more cases.

At several points in the program you will be offered the opportunity to obtain a printed copy of the results of an analysis. In addition, you may obtain a hard copy of any screen by using the print screen (PrtSc key) or (Ctrl-PrtSc keys) capability of your PC.

HINTS!! Plan your session with STAT before going near a computer. A well-thought-out plan can reduce both the time and the frustration involved. For example, you may wish to perform analyses using both the original and recoded values for a variable. Plan to do the analysis with the original values first. When this is finished, do the recoding and then the second analysis. Were you to reverse the order, you would have to read in the data file a second time to have the original values available.

You MUST understand the various techniques before attempting to employ STAT to do an analysis. STAT is like a box of tools . Just owning a screwdriver or a hammer does not enable one to tune an engine or build a house.

8.2   Subprogram Instructions

Three subprograms require more detailed instructions. These are shown below.

8.2.1   Data Modification

This program allows the user to alter the values stored for the cases in a file. There are a number of reasons one might wish to do so. No matter how carefully one plans a coding scheme, some codings may later prove cumbersome. Analyses not anticipated when the data was collected may require different codings for one or more variables. The time and effort required for data entry may be reduced. For example, if you enter cost per insertion and number of insertions for an ad, it would not be necessary to type in total cost in dollars; the two values already entered could be multiplied to find total costs.

With the Data Modification subprogram, it is possible to make changes to one's data quickly and easily. The program consists of two distinct modes, **Recode** and **Arithmetic Operations**. In both instances, the changes you make affect the values for all cases.

Changes made in this subprogram remain in effect for an entire session as opposed to changes made in Crosstabs or Frequencies. Changes in the latter remain in effect only until a new variable is specified or a new statistical procedure is selected. It is, therefore, useful to plan your analyses and recodings. Suppose you have income coded in four categories and you want to do an ANOVA or Crosstabs using all four categories and one with only two: high and low. Do the analysis with all four categories first, then recode the data and do the analysis with two categories. If you did it in the reverse order, you would have to read in the data a second time since the original detail is lost in recoding. Rereading a data file doesn't take awfully long, but it can be quite annoying.

You may make multiple passes over the data to accomplish all modifications you desire. After you have finished making changes you will be given the opportunity to save the file of modified variables on disk. Whether you save or not, you can specify new names appropriate to the modified variables. This is merely a convenience feature and, naturally, has no effect on the statistical procedures.

Modes

Recode takes some specified values and converts them to other values. Take, for example, recode 1 to 2. All cases originally coded 1 will have the value 2 after the operation. If the variable were education, 1 might indicate eighth grade or less and 2 could identify high school graduates. The result of the recoding would be a new category, high school graduate or less.

Arithmetic Operations allows you to perform computations using whatever values are stored for a variable. Perhaps for a number of cities, variable 1 is population and variable 2 is sales of your product. Dividing variable 2 by variable 1 would yield per capita sales.

Recode

Recoding involves identifying one or more values a variable now has and specifying some new code with which these will be replaced. **Recoding** is useful:

1. to correct coding errors or shortcomings. Note: you cannot add detail. If divorced and widowed were originally coded as a single category, say 3, it stands to reason that they can never be separated.

2. to combine groups of cases for analysis. For example, if you coded years of education as an integer, recoding 1 through 12 to 1 and values greater than 12 to 2 would allow you to compare those who didn't continue beyond high school with those who did.

3. to select cases to be used in the analysis. Continuing the preceding example, to run a regression for only high school graduates one could set 1 through 12 to 1 and then specify 1 as missing in the regression procedure. Those reporting education levels of high school or less would be excluded from the regression.

In recode mode, you may either a) specify an individual value which is to be recoded to some new value or b) specify a range of values to be recoded. The former alternative is self-explanatory, i.e., recode 1 to 2.

To recode a range of values you may:

1. specify both ends of a range of values to be recoded;

2. recode from the lowest value through some desired value;

3. recode from some desired value through the highest value to some new value.

Be careful about using a range if it may include missing values. They will be recoded just as any other number.

Arithmetic Operations

This mode will allow you to compute new values for an existing variable. Due to memory limitations, you cannot add additional variables to the variable set. However, any existing variable may be replaced with totally new values.

The old values are lost for the balance of the session. Data stored on the disk is not affected, so you have the option of starting over if you make an error.

The computations are done in simple steps. Complex computations can be performed in several stages.

The following abbreviations and symbols are used to describe the options:

rv	▷	resulting variable. Holds the results of the computation.
fv	▷	first variable in equation
sv	▷	second variable in equation
c	▷	a constant
+	▷	add
-	▷	subtract
*	▷	multiply
/	▷	divide
^	▷	raise to a power

For example, rv=fv*sv means multiply fv by sv and place the results in rv.

OPTIONS

1.	rv = fv + sv	5.	rv = fv + c
2.	rv = fv - sv	6.	rv = fv - c
3.	rv = fv * sv	7.	rv = fv * c
4.	rv = fv / sv	8.	rv = fv / c

exponentiation

9.	rv = fv ^ sv	10.	rv = fv ^ c
11.	exit arithmetic operations		

Remember, raising a number to a fractional exponent is the same as taking a root. For example, $4 \char`\^ 0.5 = 2 =$ the square root of 4.

8.2.2 Frequencies

The Frequencies subprogram is useful for examining the values recorded for a variable. In most marketing research applications, a Frequencies run is the first step in analyzing data. The output includes the median and mode, and a listing of the frequency with which each value occurs and cumulative frequencies. A histogram is included. If you want the mean for a variable, use the mean subprogram.

The initial listing may be sent to either the screen or a printer. If screen mode is chosen, you will have a second chance to obtain printed results. It is usually a good idea to take a look at the results on the screen first. Then when you are satisfied with the outcome of the analysis, have the results printed.

You will be required to specify a single missing value. This is the code given to "no response," "not applicable," "data not available," etc. If more than one value indicates data is missing for a case, you will have to use the recode facility before running the Frequencies procedure.

To save computing time, this routine uses positive integers in the range 0–1000. Fractional values will be rounded to the nearest whole number. This will handle all case data originally on the disk without modification.

You may wish to analyze data you have entered that exceeds this range. If so, you will have the opportunity to enter a multiplier that scales the variable to the proper range.

For example,

Range of your data	Enter multiplier	Resulting range
.001 - 1.0	1000	1 - 1000
1000 - 100000	.001	1 - 100
1000 - 1000000	.001	1 - 1000

After scaling, values are then rounded to the nearest integer. Values that are still outside of the acceptable range are set to missing. So, the following will result in values between one million and ten million being counted as missing.

Range of your data	Enter multiplier	Resulting range
10000 - 10000000	.001	10 - 1000

If these are an important portion of the range, a multiplier of .0001 would salvage these values at the expense of those between one thousand and ten thousand.

If your data contains NEGATIVE values, you can either use a negative (-) multiplier or add a constant using the recode program.

This program checks for missing data indicators *before* applying the multiplier. You do not need to try to compensate. Suppose you coded missing values as 4444 and are using a multiplier of 0.1. The missing value code remains 4444, not 444.

The Frequencies subprogram runs slower than others. Be sure to plan enough lab time if you are running a lot of variables.

8.2.3 Crosstabs

Crosstabs can develop and analyze two-way contingency tables. Each variable is limited to four levels. A recode option is included to permit analysis of continuous variables and others coded into more than four values. Crosstabs runs in two modes: **Integer** and **Recode**.

In **Integer** mode, you will be required to specify up to four integers identifying group membership (categories) for each variable. These values do not need to be sequential. They should be in ascending order. A set such as 1, 2, 70, 80 is acceptable.

Recode mode handles continuous variables. Ranges of values are recoded to integers denoting classes or categories. You will be asked to enter the code for the bottom of up to four categories and the code of the maximum value for the top category. For all categories except the last, all values greater than or equal to the bottom value of one category and less than the bottom value of the next higher category are included in the lower category.

Recode will automatically include all values between the lower bound of the lowest category and the upper bound of the largest category in the analysis. If there are values, or blocks of values in that range that you wish to exclude, the Data Modification program should be used for the recoding.

By judicious specification of boundaries (and missing values), Crosstabs can be fooled into handling some mixed designs. For example, suppose you wish to recode a continuous variable and crosstabulate it with an integer row variable originally coded 1, 2, 3, 4. Use Recode mode and specify 1, 2, 3, 4, 5, as boundaries for the row variable.

8.3   STAT: Sample Runs

Two sample runs of STAT are shown below. In the first, the user has chosen to load and analyze an existing data set as would be appropriate if one were analyzing a case or had previously stored data in a file on disk. In the second, new data is entered.

It will be extremely helpful if you study these examples carefully before using STAT. We really want to convince you that STAT is as easy to use as we say it is. In this instance, familiarity breeds not contempt, but contentment.

With three exceptions, this material is exactly as it would appear on your monitor; in fact, we merely routed the display to a printer instead of to the screen. The exceptions are: a) User responses have been boldfaced and placed in boxes, $\boxed{\mathbf{y}}$, to set them apart from the computer queries and instructions which are in smaller print inside the frames. b) Some explanatory notes have been included. These are in regular type and begin at the normal left margin. These notes will not appear on your screen. c) Several sequential screens may be shown in a single frame. Instructions and requests for input usually stand alone on a screen.

Remember, a carriage return (C/R) is almost always required to complete an entry. This is usually indicated in the computer prompt. If you feel you have done all that is required and nothing happens, press C/R to be sure. Since carriage returns will not appear on your computer screen, they are not indicated in these examples.

8.3.1   Example 1: Analyzing an Existing Data Set

In what drive will the program disk be located?

A/B/C? $\boxed{\mathbf{b}}$

Press the ESC key to go to the main menu.

The disk containing STAT is in the B drive.

The ESC key will interrupt any routine. There aren't many instances when you will want to use it. If you make a mistake, it is usually faster to let it go and enter the correct instructions when given the chance.

Press s and return to skip instructions.

? $\boxed{\text{s}}$

Is data from keyboard? enter k

       disk? enter d

          k/d? $\boxed{\text{d}}$

The user did not wish to review the instructions.
An existing data set will be read in from a disk file.

Disk Drive A/B/C? $\boxed{\text{c}}$

Name of data file? $\boxed{\textbf{test 10}}$

The disk with the data file does not need to be in the same drive as the program disk.

TEST10 is a name of a file previously saved on disk.

Check disk. Press c/r when ready.

?

C/R was pressed in response to the prompt.

The following is presented just to let you know that the correct things are happening while the computer reads in data from the disk.

      LOADING
READING CASE 1
READING CASE 2
READING CASE 3
READING CASE 4
READING CASE 5
READING CASE 6
READING CASE 7
READING CASE 8
READING CASE 9
READING CASE 10

A description of the file is given to be sure it is the right one and to refresh your memory as to its contents.

```
There are 7 variables
          and 10 cases in your file.

The variables are
     1 sex      2 married?     3 age      4 income
     5 index    6 Auto.loan$   7 mo payment

Type C/R to continue.
?

Do you want a listing of the variables?

     If yes type y.

     If no type n.
     ? [y]
```

The user indicated a desire to examine the values stored for each variable for each case. This is a good idea if you have any doubts about the accuracy of the data in the file.

```
Hit N     to advance   to next   case
Hit C     to correct
Hit S     to cease      listing

var 1     var 2        var 3     var 4     var 5   var 6         var 7
sex       married?     age       income    Index   auto.loan$    mo payment
case 1
0.00      2.00         0.00      60.00     0.00    27323.00      946.
C/N/S?    [c]
```

The user wishes to correct a value. There may have been some error in coding or data entry. The data for this case will be displayed once again to be sure.

```
                        case 1
1-sex              0.00  2-married?     2.00  3-age              0. 00
4-income          60.00  5-index        0.00  6-Auto loan$  27 323.00
7-mo payment     946.00

    Number of   variable   to be corrected   ? [1]

New value?              [1.]
```

The value of sex for this case will be replaced. Maybe 1 indicates males and 0 females. Or the reverse could be true.

The case's data, after the correction, are shown.

```
                        case 1
1-sex              1.00  2-married?     2.00  3-age              0.0 0
4-income          60.00  5-index        0.00  6-Auto loan$   273 23.00
7-mo payment     946.00

    To make    another   correction to  this case  type c
    To continue  listing  type r
    C/R?              [r]
```

No more corrections to this case.

The listing of cases will resume with the next case.

```
case 2
0.00      0.00   3.00  82.00   0.00  67662.00   540.
C/N/S?  [c]
```

Another error is detected.

```
                        case 2
1-sex              0.00  2-married?     0.00  3-age              0. 00
4-income          82.00  5-index        0.00  6-Auto loan$   67 662.00
7-mo payment     540.00

    Number of   variables  to be corrected   ? [2]

New value?              [2.]
```

```
                            case 2
1-sex                0.00  2-married?        2.00  3-age            0.0 0
4-income            82.00  5-index           0.00  6-Auto loan$  676 62.00
7-mo payment       540.00

     To make      another   correction to  this case  type c
     To continue  listing   type r
     C/R?           [r]
```

```
 Hit N   to advance  to next  case
 Hit C   to correct
 Hit S   to cease    listing

case 3
0.00     2.00       65.00    35.00  0.00  39368.00  460.
C/N/S?   [s]
```

```
Do you want to save your new or corrected data on disk y/n?
?  [n]
```

No more corrections.

The data should have been saved, but with ten cases it doesn't matter much. It won't take long to reenter if something goes wrong.

The main menu will now be displayed for the first of many times.

```
                              MENU
  1   MEAN, STANDARD DEV, CV        2   PEARSON CORRELATION
  3   SIMPLE LINEAR REGRESSION      4   FREQUENCIES, MEDIAN, MODE
  5   T-TESTS                       6   CROSSTABULATION
  7   MULTIPLE REGRESSION           8   ANALYSIS OF VARIANCE
  9   DATA MODIFICATION            10   DISPLAY INSTRUCTIONS
 11   LOAD A FILE                  12   LIST AND OR CHANGE DATA
 13   END STATISTICS

      Type your selection and C/R.        ?   [1]
```

The user selected subprogram 1.

Descriptive	Statistics:	Interval	Variables
1 sex	2 married?	3 age	4 income
5 index	6 Auto.loan$	7 mo payment	

Variable?   3

missing value?   999

Variable names are listed at the beginning of each subprogram.

Descriptive statistics will be calculated for variable 3.

Those who refused to answer this question were coded 999.

The results appear on the screen.

Variable   3

age

The mean of variable 3 is	38.20
The standard deviation is	29.30
The variance is	858.62
Good cases	10
Missing cases	0
Sum	382.00
The coeff of var (%) is	76.71

Do you want descriptive stats for
another variable?

y = yes

n = no

? n

Do you want to run another program?

y = yes

n = no

? n

That's all folks.

If user had entered $\boxed{\text{y}}$, the program would return to STAT main menu.

$$\boxed{\textbf{END STATISTICS}}$$

The user will be returned to the disk main menu.

8.3.2   Example 2: Entering New Data

```
In what drive will the program disk be located?
A/B/C? [b]

Press the ESC key to go to the main menu.

Press s and return to skip instructions.
? [s]
```

The program disk is in the B drive.

The ESC key will interrupt any routine.

The user still doesn't want to see the instructions. Must have read the text.

```
Is data from keyboard?   enter k
                disk?    enter d
                 k/d? [k]
```

The user is creating a new data set.

Entering new data.
How many cases do you have (max 225)?
If you are uncertain enter 225, then enter 1e9 after last entry.
If you want to save after every few cases enter 225 and then enter 1e9
after any complete case.

? 225

How many variables do you have (max 40)?

? 3

Press n and c/r if you do NOT wish to use descriptive variable names.
Press Y and cr to use names. y / n? y

A wise choice. Otherwise, it's easy to forget what number corresponds
to what variable.

Enter variable names of up to 10 characters at the prompt.

Name of variable 1
? age

Name of variable 2
? income per year

Name of variable 3
? sex

What's wrong here?

You may now check the names you entered.

1 age   2 income per   3 sex

Do you want corrections y/n? n

The name for V-2 was truncated because it was too long.

Wouldn't you fix the name of V-2?

The computer will prompt for each variable for each case. Data is typed in at the ? prompt. Errors may be corrected prior to pressing C/R by using the backspace key. If an error is noted after C/R is pressed, note the case and variable number and correct it when reviewing your data.

```
Enter your data casewise.
case 1
var 1 AGE
?  19
var 2 INCOME PER
?  38000
var 3 SEX
?  1
case 2
var 1 AGE
?  25
var 2 INCOME PER
?  20000
var 3 SEX
?  0
⋮
case 7
var 1 AGE
?  65
var 2 INCOME PER
?  77
var 3 SEX
?  4
case 8
var 1 AGE
?  1e9
```

User enters **1e9** to signify last case has been entered.

Do you want to save your data on disk?

Enter y for yes.

Enter n for no.
? n

The user will be sorry if someone kicks the plug.

Do you want a listing of the data?
If yes type Y.

If no type N.

? y

We've been here before.

Hit N   to advance   to next case
Hit C   to correct
Hit S   to cease   listing
var 1   var 2   var 3
age   income per   sex
case   1
19.00   38000.00   1.00 C/N/S? $\boxed{\text{n}}$

case   2
25.00   20000.00   0.00 C/N/S? $\boxed{\text{n}}$

case   3
29.00   50100.00   1.00 C/N/S? $\boxed{\text{n}}$

case   4
40.00   75000.00   0.00 C/N/S? $\boxed{\text{n}}$

case   5
45.00   49200.00   0.00 C/N/S? $\boxed{\text{n}}$

case   6
55.00   49.00   0.00 C/N/S? $\boxed{\text{n}}$

var 1   var 2   var 3
age   income per   sex

case   7
65.00   77.00   4.00 C/N/S? $\boxed{\text{c}}$

An error is detected in case 7 and will be corrected.

case 7
1-age   65.00   2-income per   77.00   3-sex   4
Number of variable to be corrected ? 3
New value? 1
case 7
1-age   65.00   2-income per   77.00   3-sex   1
To make another correction to this case type c
To continue listing type r

C/R? r

Do you want to save your new or corrected data on disk y/n?
? n

	MENU		
1	MEAN, STANDARD DEV, CV	2	PEARSON CORRELATION
3	SIMPLE LINEAR REGRESSION	4	FREQUENCIES, MEDIAN, MODE
5	T-TESTS	6	CROSSTABULATION
7	MULTIPLE REGRESSION	8	ANALYSIS OF VARIANCE
9	DATA MODIFICATION	10	DISPLAY INSTRUCTIONS
11	LOAD A FILE	12	LIST AND OR CHANGE DATA
13	END STATISTICS		

Type your selection and C/R.   ?   2

Subprogram 2 was selected.

Simple Correlations

1 age   2 income per   3 sex

Enter BOTH variable numbers separated by a comma.
? 1,2

missing value for first var? 999
missing value for second var ? 999

It is important to follow the instructions exactly. You will get a second
? prompt prior to the missing value prompt if you specify only one variable.

Many choose some value, like 999, that they always use for missing values
unless it is inappropriate in a particular instance. It simplifies keeping track.

Pearson Correlation
r = -0.478
r square = 0.229
Good n 7
Missing cases 0
Do you want to correlate
other variables?
y = yes
n = no
? ⌐y⌐

Simple Correlations
1 age   2 income per   3 sex
Enter BOTH variable numbers separated by a comma.
? ⌐2,3⌐
missing value for first var? ⌐999⌐
missing value for second var ? ⌐999⌐

Pearson Correlation
r = -0.128
r square = 0.016
Good n 7
Missing cases 0
Do you want to correlate
other variables?
y = yes
n = no
? ⌐n⌐

```
Do you want to run another program?

y = yes
n = no
?  y
```

```
                              MENU
 1  MEAN, STANDARD DEV, CV          2  PEARSON CORRELATION
 3  SIMPLE LINEAR REGRESSION        4  FREQUENCIES, MEDIAN, MODE
 5  T-TESTS                         6  CROSSTABULATION
 7  MULTIPLE REGRESSION             8  ANALYSIS OF VARIANCE
 9  DATA MODIFICATION              10  DISPLAY INSTRUCTIONS
11  LOAD A FILE                    12  LIST AND OR CHANGE DATA
13  END STATISTICS

    Type your selection and C/R.       ?   4
```

The user selected (4) Frequencies, Median, Mode.

```
          MEDIAN, MODE, RANGE, FREQUENCIES
               INITIALIZING PROGRAM

               Type I for instructions.
               Type C/R to skip.     ?
        1 age        2 income per        3 sex

               Variable number?  2

          Multiplier or C/R for default 1?  .01
      Missing value code or C/R for default 999?  999
```

The instructions that could have been requested are those for this sub-program.

```
Do you want a frequency listing? y/n?  y

Screen or printer? s/p?  s
```

Choosing n would produce a summary table.

There will be a second chance for printed output.

VAR # 2   income per

Median 380

mode   380

Press C/R to advance
?

The listing will pause after each full screen.

Value Multiplier	Freq .01	Rel freq %	Cum freq %
0	1	14.29	14.29
1	1	14.29	28.57
200	1	14.29	42.86
380	1	14.29	57.14
492	1	14.29	71.43
501	1	14.29	85.71
750	1	14.29	100.00
Total	7	100.00	100.00
missing cases	0		

Press C/R to   continue?

Do you want a   hard copy   now?
    y/n ?   [n]

The summary below would have been printed immediately if the user had not asked for a listing of the frequencies.

SUMMARY

Your multiplier was .01 .
variable # 2 name income per
380
mode 380
the range is 0 to 750

Type C/R to continue?

Do you want to run another variable y/n? [n]

Do you want to run another statistical routine y/n? [n]

[END STATISTICS]

Chapter 9

UNIVARIATE DATA ANALYSIS

9.1   Eat Easy Foods (A)

Eat Easy Foods' history, like that of many firms and families in New England and eastern Canada, spans the world's longest undefended frontier, the U.S. Canadian border. In 1890, Hiram Brownsmith inherited Brownsmith & Son, Inc., a grocery wholesaler located in Portland, Maine. The firm supplied retailers in the eastern United States north of the Boston market. Upon experiencing difficulties in purchasing canned goods at reasonable prices from packers in the Midwest and California, Hiram looked north of the 49th parallel. In 1907, he acquired Nova Canners and Packers in the Annapolis Valley, the most productive farming region of the province of Nova Scotia. Over time, the wholesale business stagnated while the cannery prospered, particularly given the Great War's demand for preserved food products.

The family and the firm relocated to Windsor, Nova Scotia in 1916. The wholesale operation became a wholly-owned subsidiary of Nova Canners, Limited.

Growth in the twenties was steady, but unspectacular. The firm was profitable, but not spectacularly so. The Brownsmith family avoided the excesses of the decade, but also failed to capitalize on any of the opportunities for growth. The dirty thirties nearly devastated the firm, given its dependence upon a single industry, food processing.

By 1938, with World War II on the horizon, the fortunes of food processors changed for the better. Having been burned by their lack of diversification during the depression, the family took the firm public, retaining a large enough holding to constitute a controlling interest.

The firm prospered handsomely during the war and the baby boom years that followed. It acquired plants in Ontario, Ohio, Michigan and California to meet burgeoning demand. Sales were concentrated in central and eastern Canada and the northeast quadrant of the United States. In the late seventies, Village Smithy, the Brownsmith family's holding company, became involved in Nova Scotia land development with NewNova, Ltd., a holding company owned by Montreal's Langile family. The Langile brothers and associated family members build, own, and, manage major office and commercial properties throughout the United States and Canada.

In 1983, for reasons too complex to explore here, Nova Packers was acquired by a Boston-based subsidiary of NewNova. The path of the merger was smoothed when the Brownsmith family agreed to exchange their shares in the food company for NewNova common stock. Minority shareholders responded readily to what was seen as a more than generous offer of NewNova preferred stock.

Never ones to forget their friends, the Langiles offered the position of president and CEO to Garth MacDonald, Nova Packers' marketing VP and heir apparent to the bulk of the Brownsmith fortune. Garth, a graduate of York University and the Harvard Business School, accepted. (He had a reputation for making his money in the old-fashioned way, by capitalizing upon personal contacts to the fullest.) While some may have viewed Garth's approach to managing his personal finance with dismay, his use of the "network" was very much in the Langile mold. They believed him to be a bright, energetic marketer whose progress within the company had been blocked by the retiring chairman and president, Hans Heinhofer. Hans was the creature of a coalition of minority stockholders and, fortunately for the Brownsmith interests, the only topic on which they could agree.

Nova Packers' progress in the past six years under Heinhofer had been steady, but far from spectacular. Market growth had stagnated given the birth dearth that followed hard upon the baby boom. Nova had achieved small increases in unit volume, but in a highly competitive environment these were extremely costly.

The profitability picture was brighter. Nova had been a leader in the shift from canned to frozen foods. They began pruning unprofitable items from their canned fruit and vegetable lines while others were still expanding theirs. Noting the rise of two-career families, Nova was among the first to introduce a line of frozen convenience foods directed at the growing numbers of time-constrained households.

9.1.1 Nova Packers' Positioning

Heinhofer's largest contribution as marketing VP and later as CEO was in identifying a market niche and establishing Nova firmly therein. He was among the first to sense the converging influences of an aging population that was more concerned with health issues, a broadly based aversion to food additives, and an accompanying desire for naturalness. Hans, upon considering the implications of these trends, developed a three-segment view of the market. At one extreme were the "health nuts." Hans, known for an appreciation of fine food, viewed this group with disdain and believed their motto to be "If it tastes good, don't eat it." Prejudices aside, Hans saw this group as a) having unstable and easily disturbed purchasing habits, b) being extremely expensive to satisfy, and c) not being substantial enough for a medium-sized firm such as Nova.

At the other extreme was the mass market. Relatively uninfluenced by health and additive concerns, this group was the target of the major food processors. Their responses to various food scares were short-lived, after which they returned rather quickly to their previous consumption patterns. Their views and behavior were drifting towards those of the middle group, but relatively slowly.

Between these two clusters in both size and intensity of feeling lay the informed middle. These consumers were concerned about health and additive issues, but avoided the extremism of the health nuts. Upscale in education, occupation and income, they tended to weigh the costs and benefits of a controversial additive and make up their own minds. Yet, given a choice between two alternatives of equal quality, one containing additives and one not, they would almost always opt for the latter. In some instances they were demonstrably willing to give a bit in quality or price (but not safety or nutritional value) to obtain additive-free products. With this "decide for myself" orientation, they tended to be heavy users of ingredient and nutrient labeling.

Hans had decided to target the middle group. Over the years Nova Packers had developed a reputation for taking an almost paternalistic interest in its customers. It capitalized upon this in a series of advertising campaigns with themes that can be paraphrased as "additives if necessary but not necessarily additives."

Those major producers who went beyond the bare minimum in content labeling suffered a credibility gap caused by the years during which they had resisted making this information available. Some critics charged that the manufacturers' new strategy was to overload the consumer with information. Simple, common language terms were never used if there was a polysyllabic chemical name available. Some consumers believed that only the companies knew for sure what went into their products and that despite long technical-sounding lists, controversial additives were routinely omitted.

Nova took a different tack. They used clear, everyday language to the greatest extent possible in their labeling. If a common language name for an additive or ingredient existed, Nova used it. If labeling laws required the technical term, Nova provided both. Regardless, Nova routinely indicated the purpose of an additive in addition to its presence. At times this detail was at the expense of the promotional aspects of the packaging; some charged that their packages looked like textbooks. Nova's target market, however, seemed to appreciate this information and responded accordingly.

9.1.2   A New Opportunity: Project Quick 'n Good

In the early eighties, Garth did some social monitoring of his own. He noted an increasing interest in food and gourmet cooking. Yet households were more time-constrained than ever. Even if both adults participated in meal preparation, there just wasn't enough time to indulge in high quality food preparation on a daily basis. The increased interest in eating was accompanied by a seemingly incompatible increase in concern for health, fitness, and slimness.

Garth conceptualized a new line of products: gourmet frozen foods. By adapting recipes from novelle cuisine, the items could truly offer a quantum quality improvement over conventional convenience items and yet still meet the demand for meals contributing to slimness and fitness. The increment in quality would be large enough and the offering unique enough to justify a substantial price premium. Nova's traditional approach to additives and labeling would be continued with these new items.

Garth engaged an outside market research supplier to investigate his idea. They conducted focus groups followed by concept tests. The results were strongly supportive of Garth's idea. Yet, when the proposal was presented to Hans, he turned thumbs down. He had operated all of his life on gut reactions and did not readily respond to research findings unless they supported his preconceptions. His success in identifying and responding to the trends of the seventies had bolstered his confidence in his own unsupported judgment. In this instance, he believed gourmet and frozen food to be mutually exclusive terms. Perhaps to justify his own rather substantial girth, he looked upon the concern with slimness and fitness as a passing fad: the Hula Hoop of the eighties.

Upon assuming the helm of Nova, Garth's first action, after appointing his assistant, Liam Kelly, to the position of acting VP marketing, was to give approval to going all out on Project Quick 'n Good. Liam had a good track record as a brand assistant with a major consumer products company, and assistant to the VP marketing at Nova. However, both he and Garth felt he needed more experience before being ready for a VP position on a permanent basis.

Further, Nova, due to its history, had a quaint, "down east" image. This proved advantageous in its consumer marketing efforts. Unfortunately, this advantage did not carry over into its relations with wholesalers and major retailers. Because of the predominance of New Englanders and Maritimers in the executive ranks, the trade saw the firm as inbred and cliquish. Competitors disparagingly referred to Nova as the Maine Mafia, or Maritime Mafia. As a result, Nova had a more difficult time than most in convincing dealers that its products would receive acceptance in the larger North American market. In one instance, a major supermarket's buying committee refused to take on a new seafood entree because they were convinced it catered only to regional tastes. In fact, the product had been developed in California by a Hispanic food technician and was based on Alaskan king crab.

Garth's appointment as president had little effect on these perceptions, since the trade had long viewed it as inevitable, only a matter of time. However, Garth and the Langiles believed that if he went outside of the firm and the region for his first major executive appointment, a significant improvement in trade relations could result. Consequently, Garth engaged a major executive recruiting (head-hunting) firm to identify candidates within the marketing ranks of major consumer package goods firms.

Garth and Liam reached a clear understanding on Liam's role during the interim period. Liam's major responsibility would be to act as director of and advocate for the Quick 'n Good line. The major reason for awarding him the title of acting VP was to emphasize the importance of that project. Garth would continue to perform many of the marketing vice president's duties.

9.1.3   Concept Tests

Liam decided he should, as a first task, personally review all of the research supporting Garth's decision to introduce the Quick 'n Good line. An outside research supplier had conducted a series of focus groups followed by concept tests. The concept tests had used a simple random sample of the population in a midwestern U.S. city frequently used as a test market. The researcher recommended and Garth agreed to in-home personal interviews so that the product concepts could be presented to respondents in written form.

In-home interviewing and the large amount of travel time required by the sampling plan raised the cost per completed interview tremendously, so the desired sample size was reduced. Interviews were completed with 50 respondents on weekday afternoons during the second week in December. Only 20 percent of those contacted agreed to participate (80 percent refusals in addition to not availables) which is quite low for this mode of data collection.

Two distinct product concepts had been tested in the research. Liam found this curious, particularly since the final report made no effort to compare or contrast the responses to the different versions. He did not want to go to the president with such a potentially trivial question. The market research director was on a business trip. A consumer analyst in the research department who remembered the sequence of events leading up to this study told the following story.

The research supplier's creative personnel could not agree on a product concept statement. They had formed two camps, each supporting one of the concepts shown in Exhibit 9.1. Nova's people did not prove to be of much assistance in resolving the issue: the research director, until recently a government economist, favored concept A, Hard Benefits. The advertising manager favored concept B, Succulence, since it was more easily translated into a creative strategy. The president of the research house, who also was a principal in the advertising agency enjoying the vast majority of Nova's billings, seemed unable to arrive at a firm recommendation, vacillating from meeting to meeting. (As the opposing camps became more locked into their positions, it became ever more likely that any clear recommendation from him would offend an influential executive within the client organization.)

Garth, always the man of action, tired of this "bickering over mere words." He adopted the position, "If we can't decide, maybe the difficulty is that these are just different ways of expressing the same product concept. Let's consider them to be equally good, use both in the field study, and get on with it." Since Garth would be paying the bill, both financially and, if the project turned into a debacle, professionally, all were glad to opt for this compromise. The two versions of the concept statement would be tested as different and coequal expressions of the same underlying idea rather than with the intention of choosing between them.

Exhibit 9.1

Concept A: Hard Benefits

Quick 'n Good products result from application of state-of-the-art food technology. The highest quality meats and produce are rushed to our plants, using costly air freight if necessary, so that they arrive on your table in the highest possible state of freshness. Our frozen entrees, full meals, and desserts are prepared under the scrutiny of our experienced staff of executive chefs. They are perfect for the busy housewife who wants to improve her family's

Exhibit 9.1 (*continued*)

---

nutrition and serve more enjoyable meals, but who lacks the time and culinary ability to pursue gourmet cooking.

Concept B: Succulence

The meals you would prepare yourself if only you had the time. A perfect solution for the modern family. We bring the best of the new cuisine to your table, courtesy of our world-class chefs. Succulent seafood, veal so white it would be lost if dropped in snow, and vegetables that arrive at your table same day fresh. Nova's Quick 'n Good line allows you to prepare gourmet delicacies while enjoying a spritzer by the fireplace rather than a stint at the stove. Eat better, not later.

Liam turned his attention to the one summary table contained in the report. Here the analysts seemed to have opted for simplicity. They had presented simple percentages and arithmetic averages rather than a lot of complicated-sounding statistics that had little meaning to the executive reader.

Exhibit 9.2. Summary of Nova Foods Study
Quick 'n Good Project

	Mean or Percent[1]	Preferred Measure
How satisfied with frozen foods on today's market[2]	3.0	_____
1 = very satisfied		
.		
.		
.		
7 = not at all satisfied		
Would buy and serve Quick 'n Good		
0 = no	22.4%	_____
1 = yes	66.6%	
Sex		
0 = male	16.0%	_____
1 = female	84.0%	
Income (000)	$38.2	_____
Age	48.3	_____
Marital Status	2.3	_____
1 = never married		
2 = married		
3 = divorced		
4 = widowed		
Children at Home	0.3	_____
0 = no		
1 = yes		

Exhibit 9.2 (*continued*)

	Mean or Percent[1]	Preferred Measure
Occupation	3.0	_____
1 = Professional/Technical		
2 = Managerial/Sales		
3 = Clerical		
4 = Craftsman (Blue Collar)		
5 = Journeymen & Apprentices		
6 = Unskilled		
0 = Not employed		
Residence	1.1	_____
1 = Central city		
2 = Inner suburb (begun before 1946)		
3 = Outer suburb		
Impression of Quick 'n Good line	3.1	_____
1 = not as good as those presently available		
2 = about equal to products now available		
3 = probably somewhat better than products now on market		
4 = a lot better than products now on market		
5 = as good as home cooked		
6 = comparable to a first quality restaurant		

[1] Values are simple averages unless % shown.
[2] Consider this to be an interval scale.

9.1.4   Case Assignment

A. Concept Writing Exercise

1. Evaluate Garth's proposal to use two concepts in order to reach a consensus all could accept.

2. Is Garth's distaste with bickering over words justified?

3. Evaluate concept A, Hard Benefits.

   (a) Strengths

   (b) Weaknesses

4. Evaluate concept B, Succulence.

   (a) Strengths

   (b) Weaknesses

5. Write a new product concept that capitalizes on the strengths and remedies the weaknesses that you have noted.

B. Sample Design

1. Evaluate the sampling plan used in the concept-testing study.

2. What alternative would you propose? Consider the state of development of the product.

3. Assume that Nova has determined that prospects for the Quick 'n Good line are households in which adult members are employed outside the home, and in which at least one adult belongs to a community or public service organization. A study of current food-purchasing habits of this target group is desired. Prepare a sampling design for this study. Do not forget:

   (a) Population

   (b) Sampling Frame

   (c) Sampling Procedure

C. Statistics

1. Are the statistics presented appropriate to the measures? If you disagree with any of the measures of central tendency, indicate your chosen measure in the space shown.

2. Load and run the STAT program on the disk accompanying this book. The data summarized in Table 1 (Exhibit 9.2) is stored as EATEASY.A. Determine the values of the statistics you listed as preferred measures in Table 1.

3. The original analysis was done using manual calculations. The analyst was later dismissed for sloppy work. Check the accuracy of the values shown using STAT.

4. A junior member of the research department commented on the "impression" question. He claimed the response categories did not constitute an interval scale and should be treated as ordinal. What is your opinion?

D. Univariate Statistics

Use an alpha of .05 for all statistical tests in this exercise. You will have to look up values in the appropriate statistical tables in your text. Fifty respondents answered each question (N = 50) unless otherwise indicated.

1. Previous research indicates the average age of Nova's customers is 48 years. Is the average age of respondents in the Quick 'n Good study significantly different? (N = 38)

    (a) This requires a _____ tailed test.

    (b) The hypotheses are:
    HO:
    HA:

    (c) What statistic is appropriate (t or z)?
    Why?

(d) Decision rule:

Accept HO if

Reject HO and accept HA if

(e) What is your decision?

2. Assume that the average household income in the test city is $15,000. Can you conclude that the respondents were below average in income? (N = 27)

(a) This requires a _____ tailed test.

(b) The hypotheses are:

HO:

HA:

(c) What statistic is appropriate (t or z)?

Why?

(d) Decision rule:

Accept HO if

Reject HO and accept HA if

(e) What is your decision?

3. The most recent census indicates that 70 percent of the employed population are in white-collar (Professional/Technical, Managerial/Sales or Clerical) occupations. Do respondents in the Quick 'n Good study differ significantly?

(a) This requires a _____ tailed test.

(b) The hypotheses are:

HO:

HA:

(c) What statistic is appropriate (t or z)

Why?

(d) Decision rule:

Accept HO if

Reject HO and accept HA if

(e) What is your decision?

4. In a number of previous studies, the response to the "Would buy and serve..." question was 40 percent yes. Is the percentage for Quick 'n Good significantly greater? (N = 26)

   (a) This requires a _____ tailed test.

   (b) The hypotheses are:

   HO:

   HA:

   (c) What statistic is appropriate (t or z)?
   Why?

   (d) Decision rule:

   Accept HO if

   Reject HO and accept HA if

   (e) What is your decision?

5. Do you believe those who responded in the Quick 'n Good study are a random sample of the general population?

   (a) Yes or no?

   (b) What are the reasons for your answer?

   (c) Assume you answered in the negative. Are there features of the sampling plan that would lead to a lack of representativeness?

Chapter 10

BIVARIATE AND MULTIVARIATE ANALYSIS

10.1   Sail A' Way (A)

Sail A' Way Rentals was located in a marina in the Florida Keys. The firm originated in 1969 when Keal Hall, a returning Vietnam veteran, invested his separation pay in a night-long exploration of the permutations and combinations of 52 objects taken five at a time. When dawn broke, Keal found himself the proud owner of the *Mary Joan*, a broken down schooner that had not been new when she was used as a rum runner during Prohibition, and a few hundred dollars cash.

Keal had had no plans upon leaving the service. Before entering, he had divided his time between sailing and devising schemes for delaying the draft as long as possible. Now, since he was a pretty fair sailor and good with his hands, he decided to see if the *Mary Joan* could earn his living. At least if he invested a little time and money in fixing her up, he could sell her for several times her present worth.

Keal quickly discovered the truth of the adage, "a boat is a hole in the water you can pour money down." His cash ran out more quickly than he expected. For the next year, he alternated between restoring the *Mary Joan* and doing pick-up jobs to pay for the required materials.

At the end of that time, he decided she was in good enough shape to start earning her keep, and began following the sun, and the tourist dollar, up and down the East Coast. He would drift into a harbor and start offering fishing charters, day charters, party cruises or anything else that was within the letter of the law. When he tired of a spot, he just weighed anchor and sailed on to somewhere else. Since his only expenses were food, gasoline for the auxiliary engine, and continued improvements on the schooner, he could get by on very little. As a consequence, he worked as much or as little as he wished.

In 1975, Keal took on Beauregarde (Beau) Baxter, a marketing student from Sunshine State University, as a hand. Noting that he had considerable time on his hands, Beau decided to try to supplement his minimum wage earnings by applying his marketing research skills to what he saw as one of Keal's major problems. This was predicting the volume of business to be generated in various ports.

When Beau proposed this idea to Keal, the latter was initially quite negative. It was perfectly clear to him that his revenues increased with the size of the city and decreased as there were more competitors for the available business. Besides, he was much less laid back when it came to those he hired. Scroogelike, he thought Beau should do whatever he was told for his fixed wage, whether that be chipping paint or doing marketing research. In the end, they agreed upon a sum which Keal swore would break him, but which was far less than the professional consulting rate Beau had felt entitled to as a third-year marketing student.

10.1.1 Data

Reflecting his casual approach to business, Keal kept few records, a fact that he had discussed with the income tax people on several occasions. The entries in his ledger were sporadic at best. At some times, he would record the revenue for the duration of his stay in a specific port. At other times, there would simply be an entry for a period of time that might cover part of the time in a harbor or the time spent working several harbors. There was no way this could be narrowed down to the type of business (cruises, charters, etc).

After giving the problem some thought, Beau decided to try having Keal rate a sample of the hundred or so ports at which he had called over the years according to revenue generated. Knowing that too much detail was not warranted, he simply had Keal classify them as low, moderate, or high in potential revenue. At first Keal didn't show much interest, but he got caught up in the spirit of the process after Beau gave the categories the fanciful titles of hagfish, cod, and mermaids.

After Keal classified a random sample of twenty, Beau went to the records. For 15 of the sample of 20 ports, Beau could check the appropriateness of the classification by comparing the financial ledger with the ship's log. Keal's ratings proved to be amazingly accurate, so they went ahead and classified the entire 103 ports at which the *Mary Joan* had called over the years.

Some atlases and nautical publications Keal kept on board contained demographic information about the various harbors and indicators of the level of competitive activity for charters and cruises. Seaboard Travel Research, the research unit of a regional tourist promotion agency, provided information on the level of tourism-related activity at the various locations.

10.1.2 Analysis

Beau recommended using crosstabulation analysis to identify relationships. Keal readily agreed, not being exactly sure what it was. Beau spent his free time for a while performing a number of analyses of the data. Most proved to be dead ends. However, crosstabulations involving the following variables proved interesting. The level of tourist activity was taken from the average daily tourist-resident ratio reported by Seaboard Travel Research for the June 1st to September 30th period. This is a widely used indicator of the intensity of tourism-related business activity.

The variables Beau collected and the codings are shown below.

- Quality of Port:

  1. Hagfish

  2. Cod

  3. Mermaid

- Level of Competition:

  1. Low

  2. Intense

- Level of Tourist Activity:

  1. Low

  2. High

- Size

  1. Small

  2. Medium

  3. Large

10.1.3   Case Assignment

This is a two-part computer exercise. To save machine time you should read the requirements thoroughly prior to beginning your computer session.

1. The data Beau assembled and analyzed is stored on the program disk as SAILA.DAT. Perform your own analyses using STAT.

    (a) What factors seem to be related to the amount of business to be realized in a harbor?

2. The results of three-way analyses of the data (which cannot be done using STAT) are stored on program disk 1. Select SAIL A from the main menu and examine these tables.

   (a) Is the statistic employed appropriate to the level of measurement?

   (b) Keal looked at these results and claimed that they confirmed his beliefs about factors related to the level of business in a harbor (size of city and competition). Do you agree?

   (c) Do these results indicate that there is a causal relationship between the intensity of tourist activity or the competitive situations and the revenue potential of a port? If not, what statistic could be used to demonstrate causation?

3. Can you fault the data actually collected? Could taking Keal's estimate of the business potential of a harbor have contaminated the results?

10.2   Sail A' Way (B)

The year 1978 marked a major juncture. By then Keal had picked up a wife and three children along the way. Pulling the kids out of their schools two or more times a year was becoming a larger and larger imposition. They and their mother were making noises about having "beds that didn't rock" with ever increasing frequency. The *Mary Joan* was in as good shape as she would ever be and just staying even would take more and more time. Maintaining didn't offer nearly the challenge of restoring. Besides, being a sail bum just wasn't the fun it used to be.

Spring 1978 found the *Mary Joan* in a small harbor between Ft. Lauderdale and Miami, provisioning for the annual odyssey north. A retired Chicago commodity trader dropped up from Miami to confirm his charter for the fall. During the discussion, he half jokingly made his oft repeated offer to buy the *Mary Joan*. This time the price was higher, the journey north seemed longer and Keal was more bored than ever with the idea of making it.

To both men's surprise, a running joke became reality; a deal was struck. Within half an hour the broker had a ship he wasn't sure what to do with and Keal was both jobless and homeless.

According to the terms of sale, half of the purchase price was paid up front. The balance was to be paid upon delivery of the vessel to a slip the trader rented in Miami. Since the purchaser wasn't particularly interested in taking possession before the end of August, Keal was faced with nothing to do and most of the summer in which to do it. He and his wife decided to spend a few months sailing around the Florida Keys and the Caribbean while making up their minds what they were going to do after turning over the *Mary Joan*. To be truthful, dissonance was setting in and their old rootless lifestyle hadn't been so bad after all.

The end of June found the *Mary Joan* sitting in Key We awaiting delivery of a small part needed to repair her navigational equipment. Key We is a small island that at low tide appears to be an integral part of Key Largo. The repair part had to come from Salt Lake City, seemingly by pack train, and Keal spent endless hours trading lies with Mort (no one knew his real name). Mort was the owner of the ship's supply store where the part had been ordered, Mort's Marina, and several other businesses on Key We and Key Largo.

Mort dominated most of the conversations, usually bemoaning the state of his businesses and the difficulty of finding good help. He knew radical changes were necessary but, due to his advancing age and the lack of personal financial necessity, lacked the drive to implement them. Keal's casual observations indicated that most of Mort's facilities certainly needed a bit of sprucing up. Whether the businesses themselves were sound, he could not tell and he had no reason to delve further into the topic.

The long-awaited part arrived on July 2nd. The *Mary Joan* left for the Cayman Islands on the following morning. After a month of exploring Caribbean islands, the *Mary Joan* was back in Key We, sitting out a storm. Mort, learning for the first time of the sale of the *Mary Joan* and realizing that Keal had a substantial amount of temporarily ready cash, broached the subject of selling some or all of his holdings in the Keys to the Halls.

Discussions continued for several days, but the two men seemed to be getting further apart. Mort became more and more convinced that he wanted to sell everything and Keal grew increasingly sure that he didn't want to spend his time and energy on anything not related to sailing. Prices on the individual properties were quite reasonable. However, Keal did not feel he could manage the financing for the whole package and simply was not interested in some of the businesses. While the layover was enjoyable, the negotiations were nonproductive and the Halls left to take the *Mary Joan* up the coast for delivery.

By mid-September Keal was climbing the walls of their rented condo and it was apparent that he would either have to find a job or lose a wife. Though he had many marketable skills, a decade of independence had left him with little inclination to go to work for someone else. He decided to drop down to Key We one more time.

A real estate developer had expressed an interest in buying Mort's souvenir shop, restaurant, filling station, motel and condos on Key Largo. The deal was in limbo because Mort still insisted that he wanted to sell all or nothing. The developer had no interest in the Key We properties.

Keal's reappearance suggested a solution and three-way negotiations began in earnest. Keal was anxious to buy the marina and ship's supply store and the sailboat rental agency. A marine and outboard engine agency and fuel supply became a bone of contention. Keal, who disliked "stink boats" didn't want it and neither did the developer. Keal finally agreed to buy it if Mort would take back a note for 75 percent of his total purchase price. A deal was worked out that all could live with.

A fresh coat of paint, a little spit and polish and one change of managers got most of Keal's new empire moving again. All were merged into a new corporate entity, Key We Enterprises, Inc. The feeling of belonging to a larger organization with new, vigorous leadership seemed to do wonders for employees of the formerly fragmented businesses. Mort's Marine Rentals, which Keal took on as his pet project, was another matter. The old hulls just didn't seem to catch the spirit.

10.2.1   Creating Sail A' Way

The rental agency had just sort of grown. Mort had loved boats of all types and couldn't resist anything that appeared to be a good buy if he had a little cash. As his "fleet" grew, he responded to the odd offer to rent one for a few days. Finally, he formalized this practice by establishing the rental agency.

Mort had bought anything that floated if the price was right because he enjoyed working on boats. As the number of craft grew larger and he grew older, Mort was no longer able to keep up with the maintenance. Unfortunately, this was one task he couldn't bring himself to hire someone else to perform, so the state of repair was miserable when Keal took charge.

Having surveyed the state of affairs, Keal decided that the good will account for the rental agency showed a negative balance; the more he could disassociate himself from the past the better. The name, Mort's Marine Rentals, was hardly one which captured the imagination. After trying some alternatives on a few friends, he settled on Sail A' Way.

All craft were given a detailed inspection and only those that were in first class shape, or could be in less than a month, were kept in the active line for the 1978–1979 season. The remainder, about half of the inventory, were retired to a boat yard on the mainland where Keal would later make repair-or-replace decisions. Those warranting repair were brought back into the line as rapidly as possible and the others were sold for whatever they would bring.

A major loan from a Miami bank allowed Keal to go full speed ahead with the repairs and to purchase replacement craft. The rental fleet was up to its previous strength for the 1979–1980 season and all were in tip top shape.

10.2.2   Expansion Time

Business boomed during the next few years. During the 1984–1985 season, Keal turned away almost as many rental requests as he booked. Having reduced the bank debt to a manageable level by channeling the cash flow from his other enterprises into Sail A' Way, Keal felt the time was right for a major expansion. His major question was what type of craft he should order.

Keal thought that the personal characteristics of customers renting different types of craft could provide some guidance. If a particular class of craft was popular with a definable group of patrons and that group was growing or declining, it would be an indicator of the desirability of increasing the number of that class in the inventory. Thanks to the requirements of his insurance company, he had detailed information on every customer since he had taken over. Often those inquiring about a rental switched from one class or make to another because of unavailability. However, both the initial request and the boat finally rented were recorded in the files. Hall felt the former better reflected the nature of demand.

Records were kept on each individual craft, no two of which were identical. Since product lines with a depth of one were not particularly useful, Keal grouped them into the three categories shown below.

- Little Boats/Day Sailers

- Medium Boats

- Big Boats

For each rental he had the following information.

> Party Size: one or two; three; over three
> Marital Status: not now married; married
> Age: 20–35; 36–60; 61 +
> Occupation: White collar; Blue collar
> Residence: coastal states; other
> Income: under $30,000; $30,000 or more
> Urban area: 0 = no: 1 = yes

Keal realized that analyzing more than 5,000 records would be a monstrous undertaking and turned the task over to a Miami marketing researcher. After examining the nature of the data, the analyst suggested that the data be analyzed using frequency counts and crosstabulation.

10.2.3   Case Assignment

Since the size of the data set exceeds the capacity of STAT, some results of the analysis have been stored on the program disk. Select SAIL B from the main menu to complete this case.

1. Given the size of the data set, how could the task of analyzing it have been made more manageable?

2. Do you agree that crosstabulation is an appropriate technique?

3. Examine the tables in SAIL B. What demographic factors are related to the type of boat chosen? How?

4. In some instances the results of two-way and three-way crosstabulations do not seem to agree. What is your explanation?

5. What criteria should be used for selecting target markets?

6. What size(s) of craft would you recommend Keal buy?

10.3 Eat Easy Foods (B)

The results of subsequent tests, of the Quick 'n Good concept with an improved study design were extremely encouraging. Nova's kitchen staff had been giving highest priority to developing items for the new line. After several waves of taste tests and in-home usage tests, the chief home economist felt three entrees, four vegetable dishes, and two desserts were ready to be offered to the public.

Meanwhile, the search for a marketing vice president had proved successful. The executive recruiters had identified five candidates who had the necessary qualifications and agreed to be considered for the position. After what seemed to be an interminable series of meetings with prospects in airport lounges and convention hotels, Garth offered the position to Bill Whitney. Until recently Whitney was a senior executive with Warner and Wager, a major consumer products company.

Bill had left his former employer with an extremely lucrative golden handshake following a dispute with the president. Careful examination of the separation agreement by expert legal minds indicated the following. Its provisions barring Bill from taking employment with competing makers of health and beauty aids or cleaning products were ironclad. However, those treating food products were very weak. There was almost no chance that a court would hold for Warner and Wager, if the firm attempted to enforce them. To clinch the deal, Garth agreed to pay Whitney's legal costs in the unlikely event that his former employer tried to sue.

Liam had mixed emotions. It had been clearly understood that he was an acting vice president. However, he had enjoyed the prestige that went with the VP marketing title. On the other hand, the Quick 'n Good project was taking an increasing amount of his time. Garth was helpful, but too many things were falling between the cracks. Further, Whitney was reputed to be a real specialist at introducing new product lines. On balance, Liam felt that working under Whitney as manager of the Quick 'n Good project was the most career enhancing thing he could do. This was true whether he stayed with Nova in the longer term or not. (Besides he would be ready to move up and would have the inside track when Bill reached mandatory retirement in three years.)

Whitney joined Nova just as the development work on the first wave of Quick 'n Good products was nearing completion. TV and magazine ads had been prepared and a media schedule was all but finalized.

Disagreement over a question of strategy arose just about as soon as

Whitney found his desk. Garth and Liam favored an immediate full scale roll out and had been operating under that assumption. Bill favored a more conservative approach. Reflecting his training on the banks of the Ohio, he insisted the product should be test marketed. Rather than overrule his new executive at the outset, Garth agreed. Columbus, Ohio, and Indianapolis, Indiana, were chosen as sites for the tests.

Liam, who felt the Quick 'n Good line was his baby, was deeply disappointed by the delay and apparent lack of enthusiasm. He insisted that the test-market introductions be supported by twice the budgets envisioned for these markets in the full-scale roll out plan. "Give the line a fighting chance." Whitney overruled him on this issue also.

10.3.1   Case Assignment

1. In general, what factors favor test marketing rather than going straight to a fullscale roll out?

2. What factors indicate that test marketing is undesirable?

3. Weighing these factors and the situation in the Nova case, with whom do you agree, Whitney or Garth and Liam?

4. What problems can arise when two test markets are chosen?

5. Do you agree with Liam's proposal for doubling advertising weight in the test markets?

6. Given sales results from a test market, how could you project these to a full-scale roll out?

10.4 Eat Easy Foods (C)

The Quick 'n Good introduction into test markets began the first week in September. Trade promotion had begun two months prior to insure that the product was on the shelves by the time consumer advertising was broadcast. In contrast to some previous introductions, Quick 'n Good really seemed to catch the imagination of the salesforce servicing these two areas. Test marketing was not very common at Nova.

By mid-October everyone associated with Quick 'n Good was elated. Product shipments into the test market had exceeded expectations by 30 percent. Bill Whitney was the lone *GRUMPY* (*GR*own *U*p *M*ature *P*erson). He expressed reservations about the degree to which shipments to wholesalers and retailers indicated product success and suggested a consumer survey to get a feel as to how the introduction was proceeding.

Garth felt that Bill was showing a lack of enthusiasm for the second time in a very short while and made this plain to Whitney. However, he was soon persuaded that they should not jump to conclusions based on insufficient information. Such conclusions all too often colored executives interpretation of the final data when it was available. Whitney was of the opinion that they should either a) reserve judgment until the test market had run its assigned course or b) commission a survey to learn what was happening at the consumer level. The latter course had the advantage of permitting the firm to modify or abort the test market if substantial weaknesses were identified. When presented in this light, Bill's position no longer struck Garth as overly cautious; in fact, it seemed eminently sensible.

Goodwork, Inc., of Cincinnati was commissioned to survey consumers in the test markets. The study objectives, in order of importance, were to determine:

1. what proportion of the market had tried the Quick 'n Good products.

2. what proportion of those trying Quick 'n Good made a repeat purchase.

3. demographic characteristics of triers and repeaters.

4. how satisfied consumers were with the products they had tried.

5. how triers had learned of the Quick 'n Good line.

Cliff Gibson, the senior analyst who directed the study, felt that the nature of the Quick 'n Good line made it particularly important that the true sponsor identity be disguised. Several alternative approaches were discussed. The parties involved finally decided to take advantage of the fact that two additional lines of frozen foods had been introduced in the two test markets that fall. Both involved minor modifications of existing lines, one by North America's largest food processor and one by a regional producer with a very substantial market share in the Midwest. Both had been given all of the hoopla of major new product introductions.

Gibson recommended that all three lines be given equal attention in the study with the sequence of questioning randomized to control order effects. Nova's research director objected that this would drastically limit the number of questions that could be asked about each line. Gibson managed to convince everyone concerned that, in this instance, it was imperative that respondents not be told, or given cues as to the true sponsor. The ability to compare Quick 'n Good to its competitors might facilitate insights that compensated for the limited number of questions about Nova's line.

Garth had previously been convinced that a telephone survey would be the best because of the desire to get the information quickly. Data was collected on four consecutive evenings during the third week in October.

A computer program was used to generate individual questionnaires and record and instantly tabulate responses. The questions and response categories are shown in the following section. Branching instructions and probes are shown, though this was handled by the computer routine. Numbers shown are for discussion purposes only.

10.4.1   Quick 'n Good Questionnaire

Introduction: (Interviewer solicits cooperation and asks to speak to the individual who normally does the food shopping.)

(If unavailable, try to get person answering to indicate a convenient time. Record, thank person on phone and terminate.)

1. Do you sometimes buy frozen prepared foods at your food store?

   (Probe on No response: "Never? Most people do, at least occasionally.")

   (If No persists, thank respondent and terminate.)

2. Have you noticed any new brands or product lines in the past couple of months?

   (Probe if respondent does not mention Q 'n G, National and Regional.)

"How about ?"

(If respondent recalls Q 'n G with or without probe go to 3.)

The following questions were asked for each brand. The ordering of brands was randomly determined by the computer.

3. Have you purchased Quick 'n Good Products?

   Which ones?

4. About how many times have you purchased Quick 'n Good?

   (On Don't Know response, probe "More than once?" "Only once?")

5. In general, how do you feel about the Quick 'n Good products you have tried? I would like you to select one of the categories I read.

   1. Delighted

   2. Pleased

   3. Mostly satisfied

   4. Mixed (about equally satisfied and dissatisfied)

   5. Mostly dissatisfied

   6. Unhappy

   7. Terrible

6. How did you first hear of Quick 'n Good?

   1. Newspaper: article

   2. Newspaper: weekly supermarket ad

   3. Newspaper: other (Nova) ad

   4. Magazine: article, feature, story

   5. Magazine: ad

   6. Radio: feature, story

   7. Radio: ad

   8. TV: feature, story

   9. TV: ad

   10. Ad in store

   11. Just saw in store freezer section

12. Received coupon in mail

13. Recommended by a friend or relative

(After questioning about all three brands:)

Now, just a few statistical questions to help us interpret your answers.

7. What is your marital status?

   1. Never married

   2. Now married

   3. Divorced

   4. Widowed

8. What is your occupation? (recorded verbatim)

9. What is your spouse's occupation? (recorded verbatim)

10. How far did you go in school?

11. How far did your spouse go in school?

	Respondent	Spouse
High School or Less (1)	___	___
Some Post Secondary (2)	___	___
College Grad (3)	___	___
Graduate or Professional School (4)	___	___

12. Approximately what is your monthly household income, before taxes?

13. Record respondent's sex.

10.4.2 First Results

Cliff was committed to having a detailed analysis of all data for all product lines performed by Goodwork's data processing department. However, that couldn't be initiated for a week and would take another week or ten days to complete and report, given the firm's workload. Cliff was meeting with Garth and Nova's research director on Monday and thought it would be politic to have some quick-and-dirty results to discuss at that time. Since he had a statistical package for his micro at home, he took a little time to recast the Quick 'n Good data into a form which would allow him to analyze it over the weekend.

Since his micro package could handle only ten variables, he selected only those respondents who answered yes to questions 1 and 2.

Questions 3 and 4 were collapsed into a single variable, V-5. The names of the variables are shown in boxes.

Variables and Codings

V–1 Sex `sex`

   0 = Male

   1 = Female

V–2 Marital Status (coded as shown above). `marital.st`

V–3 Education: the highest attainment for either partner was coded using the categories shown in the questionnaire. `education`

V–4 Occupation: The highest status occupation reported for either partner was coded using the categories shown below. `occup.cat`

   1. Professional, technical

   2. Managerial, professional sales

   3. Clerical, retail sales clerks

   4. Craftsmen & foremen

   5. Skilled trades

   6. Unskilled

   7. Other (houseperson, student, etc.)

V–5 Purchases of Quick 'n Good. `trial.qng`

   0 = never

   1 = trial, no repeat

   2 = times purchased = 2

   3 = times purchased = 3, etc.

V–6 Satisfaction (coded as shown above). (This scale is usually taken to be an interval measure.) satisfact

V–7 First learned of Quick 'n Good. (coded as shown above) learn.1st

V–8 Residence (coded from telephone number). residence

    0 = central city

    1 = suburb

V–9 Income: weekly income in hundreds. income

V–10 Occupational Status (This is an interval scale based on exact occupation reported. Each occupation is assigned a status score in the range 1–100). occup.int

10.4.3 Case Assignment

A. Bivariate Statistics

REMEMBER, correlation does NOT establish causation.

Cliff's data is stored on disk as EATEASY.C. Use STAT to analyze the data and answer the following questions. Missing data is coded 999 for all variables.

Be particularly cautious about the assumptions as to level of measurement required by the various techniques. (Hint: do not forget the recode facility. Remember, you cannot add new variables.)

1. What demographic variables are associated with trying Quick 'n Good?

2. What demographic variables are associated with repeat purchase? Think! What constitutes a REPEAT purchase?

3. Are information sources related to the probability of purchase or re-purchase?

4. Do males and females differ on any variables?

5. What sort of summary statements about Quick 'n Good's market penetration can you make?

6. Develop three hypotheses based on your beliefs about the relationships among the variables collected in the Quick 'n Good study. Record these in the space provided. Test these propositions using STAT.

H0:

HA:

Test/Statistic

H0:

HA:

Test/Statistic

H0:

HA:

Test/Statistic

B. Multivariate Statistics

1. Is satisfaction with Quick 'n Good related to:

   (a) the level of income?

   (b) occupational status?

2. What sort of relationship would you predict between satisfaction and number of purchases? Is your prediction supported by the results of the survey?

3. Make all of the interval-scaled variables available as independent variables in a regression analysis with number of purchases as the dependent variable.

   (a) What is your regression model?

   (b) What variable contributes most to explaining variation in purchases?

   (c) What variable contributes least?

4. How could you add education (V-3) or occupation (V-4) to the model?

5. Develop a regression model explaining number of purchases by those who have made at least one purchase.

6. Does residence (V-8) or occupation (V-4) appear to be related to the level of income?

7. Why would factory shipments be a misleading indicator of consumer response to the Quick 'n Good line?

10.5 Trident Theater Company (A)

The Trident Theater Company is located in Seaside, an Atlantic coastal city of 100,000. Seaside is the central city in a compact metropolitan area of 300,000 residents. It is located at the head of Seaside Harbour, one of the world's greatest natural seaports. Seaside is the port of entry for container cargos destined for destinations as far away as central Canada and Chicago.

While having little in the way of manufacturing industries, Seaside is a governmental, financial, medical, and commercial center. The surrounding region is characterized by extractive industries based on the fishery, forests, and less than abundant mineral resources. As in most areas dependent upon primary industries, unemployment is high, employment is highly seasonal, and wages are substandard when compared to the rest of the country. The lone exception is the Maryknoll valley, a one-hour drive to the south. Maryknoll is a highly productive agricultural region when compared to most of the northern Atlantic coast.

Government, hospitals, several educational institutions, including a major regional university, and a nearby military base provide a high level of stable, well-compensated employment. The financial and commercial sectors also offer considerable stability and well-paying jobs. As in many similar situations, incomes in Seaside are dichotomized between a well-educated, well-paid managerial and professional elite, and lower paid employees in clerical and operative positions in the various service industries.

Because of the unique employment mix, the former (upper and upper middle incomes) constitute a larger portion of the population than is the case in similar-sized cities that are dependent upon a manufacturing base. As a result, Seaside is a far more attractive market than population alone would suggest for sellers of upscale products ranging from luxury automobiles to concerts, lecture series, and nonfiction books.

Trident Theater Company, founded in 1973, is housed in a renovated 19th-century theater building in Seaside's historic shopping and restaurant district. Trident is one of a number of regional companies whose reputation has spread throughout North America. While it is not a repertoire company, the typical cast features one or two well-known artists, the balance of the cast being drawn from a large and relatively stable pool of local talent. Most productions are directed by Trident's artistic director who is usually an individual of international renown as a director and as an actor.

The typical season, set by the artistic director with input from the theater's board of directors and its subscribers, involves a balancing of diverse and conflicting interests. Theater goers, and the public in general, prefer elaborate productions, classics, and the works of well-known playwrights. A Broadway musical will almost automatically result in waiting lists for all available tickets. Unfortunately, given production costs and the ticket price situation (below), this "success" is realized at a financial loss.

Critics and the artistic community call for lesser known works that may educate the populace as to what's on the cutting edge of the theater world. These are often translations of obscure foreign authors, not well known outside of a select group of theater professionals. Governmental and foundation granting bodies of a nationalistic bent demand preference be given to new or recent plays by native born writers.

10.5.1   Revenue Sources

Trident derives its revenues from four sources. They are, in order of importance, a) box office receipts, b) government and foundation grants, c) corporate donations, and d) fund-raising activities.

Box Office

The source most visible to the general and theater-going public is ticket sales. The vast majority are sold to season subscribers (80 percent of total season capacity). An average season seat for five performances is priced at about $70. The theater is small (550 seats) and there is hardly a bad seat in the house according to the business manager, Fred Whitcombe. During its most recent season, the theater averaged selling 91 percent of available seats. Ticket sales account for about 48 percent of total revenue.

There is little variation in the price of seating. Whitcombe believes that over time people gravitate to seats they like and that there is little need for differential pricing. "People choose the upper balcony because they like the view or the easy access to the wine bar at intermission, not because it's a few dollars cheaper." There are larger differentials by day of the week, though Whitcombe also views these with suspicion. "Charge one price for all performances. Let them begin on the off nights and move to prime times as they earn seniority as subscribers over the years. After all, we're the only game in town."

A large number of the season tickets are sold to individuals ordering for a larger group; the average number of tickets per order is 3.43. The company requests, and usually receives the names of all persons for whom tickets are

purchased on any given subscription. The purported reason for this is so
that all patrons can be notified of schedule changes or cancellations. The
real purpose is to generate a comprehensive mailing list (the full list) of
regular theater goers rather than one limited to the individuals physically
placing an order (the short list).

At annual renewal time, the first mailings go only to those actually placing a subscription order in the previous year (the short list) and suggests
that they renew the subscription for their party. Only if no response is
received after two mailings are others named on the previous subscription
solicited directly. This procedure was adopted for two reasons. First, it
was believed to inject a personal touch, conveying the impression that Trident knew who its patrons were and how they preferred to buy. Second, it
minimized mailing costs, a not inconsequential consideration, given soaring
postal rates. The full list was only used for the semiannual benefit dinners
and to announce occasional additions to the season which were available for
an additional fee.

Grants

The second major revenue source was government and foundation grants
which together accounted for 37 percent of Trident's revenues. Foundations
were believed to favor start-up and capital-fund contributions over routine
operating grants. "Something that will rate a bronze plaque." It was fore-
ordained that Trident's income from this source would decline over time.

Government arts granting agencies were feeling the pressures for deficit
reduction, as were all other government bodies. Under the most optimistic
of forecasts, government grants were predicted to be fixed in current dollars
and declining in real terms.

A Rock and a Hard Place.   Given near-capacity houses at current
prices and a relatively affluent theater-going population, most marketers
would have suggested an increase in ticket/subscription prices as a means of
meeting rising costs. However, Trident's managers had to confront political
reality. Those administering government arts grants saw "bringing affordable
theater to the poor folk out in the hinterland," (as opposed to art for art's
sake) as a major function of their grant dollars. In an environment of fiscal
restraint, grants could not be increased to cover the deficit between costs
and ticket revenue. It was widely believed that the bureaucrats had adopted
a policy of using the grants as a club; an additional dollar of ticket revenue
would very quickly result in a lost government dollar.

Those administrators willing to admit that there was some truth in this claim justified the position on economic grounds. Fixing the total of ticket and grant revenue forced recipients to pursue internal efficiency and cost reduction—get the fat out—to make ends meet. In fact, these savings were difficult to achieve year after year and, after some initial successes, theater companies were quickly forced to tap additional sources of funds.

Corporate Donors

Corporate donations, which have grown at about the rate of inflation, account for about 10 percent of revenues. These come from a small handful of companies that contributed start-up monies back in the early seventies. Senior executives of these firms, or their wives, have been members of the company's board ever since. Though they have largely departed from the scene, the "old guard" tended to regard Trident as their personal project and resisted the involvement of other firms, even as donors. The theatre has never had a campaign to attract new corporate supporters.

Benefit Dinners

Various fund-raising events account for 5–7 percent of annual revenues. Most important are the semiannual benefit dinners. These grew out of spontaneous gatherings of subscribers during the holiday season and on the third Saturday in April, one week after the final performance of the season. Sophie, of Sophie's South Street Cafe, noted a growing number of theater patrons dining in her three-star establishment on these occasions.

Sophie didn't view this as great business. To avoid appearing ostentatious, people tended to order more frugally on these occasions than if they had simply come in on their own for dinner. They lingered over coffee and showed more interest in talking than in the bar. On the average, they cost Sophie one sitting, but she was hesitant to hurry them since many were regular patrons. As Sophie's was popular with holiday diners and April conventioneers, these gatherings were held at a loss. The staff also had begun to complain. They served fewer customers and gratuities were figured to the penny at times when the restaurant could easily have been filled with free spenders.

After this had gone on for several years, Sophie had an idea and discussed it with Trident's business manager. Under her plan the outings would be institutionalized under the theater's sponsorship. Sophie's catering service would serve a meal from the restaurant's menu that would work well with a large group. The meal would be provided at cost and the theater could sell the tickets for at least the normal retail price of the dinner, the profits going into Trident's general operating revenues. The catering service had excess kitchen capacity and could staff the event from a large and willing pool of part-time student employees. Add a little entertainment by cast members who would be glad to have the additional work and you had a real event.

This worked out to be an "everyone wins" solution. Theater goers got an event instead of a casual and unfocused evening. Trident enjoyed a significant addition to its revenues. Students and talent could earn a little much needed income. Most important to Sophie, she rid herself of unwanted patronage without offending valued customers.

This symbiotic relationship continued for four years. Last year, Sophie retired and the catering service and restaurant were sold to different buyers. The new owners of the catering service notified the theater that they could no longer serve these dinners at cost. Rather than accept a reduction in the net, Trident sought another supplier. They contracted with Moose Foods, who had taken over the feeding operation on several university campuses, to serve the meals for 30 percent less than Sophie had charged.

The winter event was fully subscribed, as always. Most seemed to enjoy themselves as usual. Some, however, were heard to complain about the quality of the food. Whitcombe felt these were representative of a new breed of chronic malcontents he was encountering with ever-increasing frequency in matters related to the theater company. In his opinion, "Everyone knows something like this is a benefit and expects 'rubber chicken.' Why would we be able to give tax receipts if they were really getting a meal worth anywhere near the cost of the ticket." Sales of tickets for the April event fell about 15 percent short of expectations.

Until this year, there had been no other organized fund-raising programs. There was a mechanism whereby those making contributions received acknowledgment in the performance programs. However, this relied almost entirely on the initiative of the donor. The theater company had devoted almost no effort to stimulating contributions.

10.5.2 A Try at Fund Raising

Having ended last season in the red, the board of directors had concluded that they must find new sources of revenue if Trident was to survive in its present form. After considering several alternatives, they decided that an appeal to current patrons was in order. After all, they were the direct beneficiaries of the company's offering. Since theater goers enjoyed quality live entertainment at a fraction of its full cost, they should be willing to help out.

The board was very sensitive to local concerns over the proportion of charity donations that went to pay for advertising and other fund-raising expenses. Consequently, they decided upon a simple straightforward request for donations printed on the bottom of the annual subscription form. Those wishing to contribute were asked to include a check along with their annual ticket order.

The appeal came to the attention of a top local radio station. Wishing to overcome image problems associated with his Top Forty format, the manager decided to "do something for the arts." He arranged for members of Trident's board and the artistic director to be interviewed by popular DJs concerning the company's current financial difficulties. He also allowed a set of really professional 30-second spots to be broadcast at times far more desirable than those usually available for public-service announcements.

The response was far less than desired; in a word, it was dismal. Fewer than 5 percent of those receiving subscription notices responded to the appeal. The contributions that were received tended to be in the $5 to $10 range. As one board member groused, "We would have done better passing the hat at a single performance."

The board was about evenly divided between those who concluded that stimulating individual donations was not a viable strategy and those who felt that the strategy was sound, but that they had made tactical errors. An individual in the latter camp managed to find a corporate donor (if the truth were known, he called in a favor) who made a contribution restricted to investigating the feasibility of stimulating individual donations and the reasons for the failure of the recent attempt.

To Market To Market, Inc., a Seaside-based marketing consulting firm with a national reputation, offered to conduct the study for out-of-pocket costs and unrestricted use of the data and findings. (The firm saw charitable fund raising as a potential growth area and believed that a successful Trident project would enhance their credibility in the field.) Trident's management and board readily agreed since this offer effectively magnified their research dollars many times.

10.5.3   Case Assignment

1. Do you believe Trident has problems other than increasing nonticket revenues?

2. Can you suggest alternatives other than a program for stimulating annual contributions by theater goers that would help solve Trident's problems?

3. Develop hypotheses or research questions concerning the cause for the failure of Trident's fund-raising appeal.

4. You have just been assigned to the Trident account by the president of To Market. Design a study to investigate your responses to the preceding item.

10.6   Trident Theater Company (B)

After discussions with the board and the principals, To Market To Market recommended that minimum attention be given to the failure of the previous fund-raising attempt. A quick-and-dirty telephone survey of twenty nondonors indicated that none of them had even been aware that Trident had attempted to solicit its subscribers for funds. Given the problems with that effort, it seemed best to write it off as a lost cause and hope that as few as possible would remember it.

Isadore Yates, the research director, recommended a study investigating the attitudes of both subscribers and nonsubscribers. She recommended surveying nonsubscribers for several reasons. First, it was felt to be important to determine whether patrons' attitudes towards giving in general and giving to Trident specifically were unique or typical of a larger population. Second, those not presently subscribing to the theater's season might do so in the future. Finally, an appeal to the general population might prove viable.

Trident's board was cold towards the notion of surveying nonsubscribers. They felt that the subscribers were the real target and that they were far from a random selection of the general population. Seaside theater goers tended to be better educated than the average and upscale in occupation and incomes. A limited number of locations within the metropolitan area housed the vast majority. A large proportion were associated with the universities or the government and private research labs located in the city.

After several discussions, Yates and the board reached a compromise; they would survey subscribers and a matched sample of nonsubscribers. Subscribers randomly drawn from the full mailing list would make up about three quarters of those surveyed. A smaller matched sample of nonsubscribers would be generated using the nearest neighbor technique.

The nearest neighbor approach is useful when one is interested in determining how those sharing some characteristic, such as subscribing to Trident, differ from people with similar demographics who do not share the characteristic. The assumption is that those living in close proximity to one another are, generally, similar in broad demographic characteristics. It is appropriate when, as is generally the case, the housing stock is made up of a number of internally homogeneous neighborhoods or areas. It works poorly when building codes or other factors result in heterogeneous neighborhoods.

In this implementation, the starting point was the list of addresses for the sample of patrons. (Taking each address, a research assistant entered the Seaside Street Guide). Having located the subscriber's address in the guide, the assistant added a small (positive or negative) random number to determine an address at which a neighbor would be interviewed. Rigid rules governed multiple family dwellings, replacements for empty lots or missing numbers, and the finding of a subscriber at the nearest neighbor address.

Yates had already decided to use a self-administered questionnaire and a drop-off/pick-up method of delivery. General areas of questioning included: a) awareness of Trident's sources of funds, b) beliefs about the need for additional funding, c) willingness to contribute funds, d) preferred mode of contributing, e) preferred timing of contributions, and f) attitudes concerning events and activities. Standard demographics were collected.

10.6.1 Case Assignment

The Trident questionnaire is shown below. The authors' explanations and comments are set off by a ⬚ box ⬚. The data collected in the Trident study is stored on the program disk as TRIDENT.DAT. Variable numbers and names are as shown in **bold face** in the questionnaire. Missing values are coded 999.

Consider Trident's problems and the general areas of questioning outlined above. Develop concrete research questions and a plan of analysis that will enable you to answer them. Use STAT to analyze the data. Develop answers to your research questions and those shown below.

1. From past experience with this type of study, Yates had set an upper limit of 40 questions. Given that Trident Theater is the client, is asking questions about the symphony and the dance company justified?

2. How accurate are respondents' perceptions about the sources of funds of the three arts organizations?

3. Do respondents' believe Trident should receive additional funds?

4. What mode of raising funds seems most promising?

5. What type of questioning was used to investigate timing of appeals? Is this appropriate?

6. What have you learned from your analyses that could be useful to Trident management in designing future fund-raising efforts?

Trident Questionnaire

> Introduction describing study as investigating attitudes towards
> cultural organizations and pledging the researcher's first born as
> an assurance of strictest confidentiality.

How important do you feel each of the following is to the quality of life
in this community? Please indicate your opinion by placing an "X" on the
line under each organization.

Seaside Symphony **1. SYM QOL**

0	100
Not at all	Extremely
Important	Important

Trident Theater **2. TRI QOL**

0	100
Not at all	Extremely
Important	Important

Blitznkoff Dance Company **3. BLI QOL**

0	100
Not at all	Extremely
Important	Important

> Note: on the graphic scales above, respondents were presented
> with a 100 mm line. Responses were coded to the nearest mm by
> measuring the distance of the mark from zero.

How frequently do you normally purchase tickets or attend performances by the following organizations.

	Less than Once a Year	About Once a Year	More than Once a Year but not a Subscriber	Season Sub-scriber
Trident Theater **4. ATTEND TRI**	(1)	(2)	(3)	(4)
Seaside Symphony **5. ATTEND SYM**	(1)	(2)	(3)	(4)
Blitznkoff Dance Company **6. ATTEND BLI**	(1)	(2)	(3)	(4)

Do you feel that the following deserve support from public or private gifts or donations?

Trident Theater (0)— No (1)— Yes **7. T DES SPT**

Seaside Symphony (0)— No (1)— Yes **8. S DES SPT**

Blitznkoff Dance Company (0)— No (1)— Yes **9. B DES SPT**

What portion of their funds do you believe each of these organizations receives from the sources shown?

Indicate a percentage for each organization for each source of funds. Percentages should total 100 percent.

	Ticket Sales %	Benefits or Events %	Government/ Foundation Grants %	Corporate Gifts %	Private Gifts %
Trident Theater	——	——	——	——	——
	10.TTIC	11.TBEN	12.TGVT	13.TCOR	14.TPRI
Seaside Symphony	——	——	——	——	——
	15.STIC	16.SBEN	17.SGVT	18.SCOR	19.SPRI
Blitznkoff Dance Company	——	——	——	——	——
	20.BTIC	21.BBEN	22.BGVT	23.BCOR	24.BPRI

Assume that Trident Theater really needed additional funds and that all sources other than private individuals had been exhausted. Choose a number from the following eleven-point scale to indicate how likely you would be to respond to the sorts of appeal shown below.

11. Certain, practically certain (99 chances in 100)
10. Almost sure (9 in 10)
9. Very probable (8 in 10)
8. Probable (7 in 10)
7. Good possibility (6 in 10)
6. Fairly good possibility (5 in 10)
5. Fair possibility (4 in 10)
4. Some possibility (3 in 10)
3. Slight possibility (2 in 10)
2. Very slight possibility (1 in 10)
1. No chance, almost no chance (1 in 100)

a. General appeal for donations. — **25. GEN APP**

b. Help sponsor a special performance such as a musical. — **26. SP PERF**

c. Attend a benefit dinner or a similar event. — **27. ATT BEN**

d. Contribute to a "Star in Residence" program bringing in nationally known talent for a play or musical. — **28. STAR SPT**

e. Contribute to a campaign to raise money for improvements to the physical facility such as reupholstering seats or installing carpet. — **29. PHYS IMP**

In the last year did you attend:

Blitznkoff's "Dance for the Survival
of Dance" performance in November?   (0)—— No   (1)—— Yes

Trident's benefit dinner in December?   (0)—— No   (1)—— Yes

Seaside Symphony's benefit concert in
March?   (0)—— No   (1)—— Yes

Trident's benefit dinner in April?   (0)—— No   (1)—— Yes

These questions were coded with the variable **30. Attend**
using the following abbreviations.

B = Blitznkoff Event; S = Symphony Event; SB = Both S & B;
TRI = Trident; APR = April; DEC = December; BO = Both

---

0. None	10. B ONLY	20. S ONLY	30. S & B ONLY
1. TRI DEC	11. B&TRI DEC	21. B&TRI DEC	31. SB&TRI DEC
2. TRI APR	12. B&TRI APR	22. B&TRI APR	32. SB&TRI APR
3. TRI BO	13. B&TRI BO	23. B&TRI BO	33. SB&TRI BO

In what month are people most likely to respond to requests for charitable donations? **31. month** _____

(January–December numbered 1–12)

Now, would you answer a few questions to help us understand our results? Again, your answers will be held in strictest confidence.

Sex   M___ (1)   F___ (2)   **32. SEX**

Marital status   (1)___   Single (Never Married) **33. MARSTAT**
                     (2)___   Now Married
                     (3)___   Divorced
                     (4)___   Widowed

What is your occupation? _____

What is your spouse's occupation? _____

Occupation of respondent and spouse were coded into the following variables.

---

34. MALEOCC	**35. FEMOCC**
(1)___ Professional and Technical	(1)___ Professional and Technical
(2)___ Managerial	(2)___ Managerial
(3)___ Clerical	(3)___ Clerical
(4)___ Foremen and Skilled Craftsmen	(4)___ Foremen and Skilled Craftsmen
(5)___ Operatives and Laborers	(5)___ Operatives and Laborers
(7)___ Houseperson, etc.	(7)___ Houseperson, etc.

How far did you go in school? _____

How far did your spouse go in school? _____

Education for respondent and spouse were coded into the following variables.

36. MALEED

(1)____ High School or Less
(2)____ Some College or Technical School
(3)____ College Graduate
(4)____ Graduate or Professional School

37. FEMED

(1)____ High School or Less
(2)____ Some College or Technical School
(3)____ College Graduate
(4)____ Graduate or Professional School

In what year were you born? ____ **38. AGE**

What was your household income after taxes last year? ____
39. INCOME

Chapter 11

FORECASTING AND MARKETING TESTING

11.1   Arctic Telephone Case

Arctic Telephone Ltd. had been experimenting with promotions and special discount plans in an effort to stimulate residential long-distance telephoning within its market. It had been determined that 65 percent of all long distance calls were 5 minutes or less and that 85 percent were less than 10 minutes. Management felt that a large number of these calls could be extended to 10 minutes if the caller was given enough incentive. A special discount was proposed that would give customers a free 5 minutes of long distance after they talked for 10 minutes. It was hypothesized that people who normally talked 5 to 10 minutes would stay on the phone a full 10 minutes to gain the free 5 minutes. The revenue gained from the extra minutes charged would more than cover the cost of providing the free 5 minutes. One drawback to the plan was that people who would normally make calls over 10 minutes might spend the same amount on the calls and simply talk longer.

Extending the length of call was particularly appealing to the telephone company. If successful, it was one of the few ways it could raise revenues to cover increasing costs without having to resort to the normal regulatory procedure of increasing long-distance rates. It was felt that the demand for long distance was relatively inelastic. With a special discount such as this, the consumer would benefit by obtaining free minutes while the telephone company would benefit from increased revenue.

The increased revenue would have to offset losses of three sorts. First, people who would normally talk 10 minutes or more anyway, and did not increase the length of their call because of the discount, would cost the telephone company up to 5 minutes in lost revenue. Second, people might talk longer, but call less often. And third, people might switch from calling in the daytime to calling in the evening or night in order to take advantage of the special discount. Not only would the telephone company be losing revenue from the free 5 minutes, but the remaining minutes of the call would normally have been charged at the 50 percent higher daytime rate.

The long-distance price structure was designed to maximize the use of the telephone system by offering lower prices during those times of the day when demand was low. The peak demand was usually during the business day so the standard rate applied from 8 a.m. to 6 p.m., Monday to Saturday (see Exhibit 11.1). Residential demand was highest Sunday from 8 a.m. to 6 p.m. and every evening from 6 p.m. to 10 p.m. when long distance was offered for one third off the business-day rate. Nights (10 p.m. to 8 a.m.) were less popular so the discount was one half off the business day rate.

Exhibit 11.1

Long Distance Discount Structure for Arctic Telephone

Discount Period

	Daytime	Evening	Night
Day of Week	8 a.m. - 6 p.m.	6 p.m. - 10 p.m.	10 p.m. - 8 a.m.
Weekdays & Saturday	Full rate	1/3 off	1/2 off
Sunday	1/3 off	1/3 off	1/2 off

Senior management decided to try the discount for one year to determine its potential for increasing long-distance revenues. They saw three distinct and independent functions that had to be performed and assigned them to the appropriate departments. The advertising department designed a special advertising campaign to be run during the offer to explain the discount to the public. The forecast department was assigned the task of determining the profitability of the discount offer. In response, they developed special forecasts of long-distance calls and minutes for the evening and night discount periods assuming no discount. This would allow them to compare the actual usage figures to the forecast figures, in order to determine the impact of the discount.

The marketing research department was assigned the task of assessing the consumers' response to the discount offer and the advertising campaign. Consequently, they made plans to survey residential customers when the special discount offer was near its completion.

The offer came into effect September 1984 and the forecast department began issuing monthly estimates of the offer's impact on revenue. The consumers' response to the offer was immediate, with increases in total minutes for both the evening and night discount periods. In October there was also an increase in the number of calls made during the evening. However, while the callers were talking more they were also spending less and, based on analysis of the first three months' data, the forecast department recommended in December that the offer be discontinued immediately.

The marketing department requested the discount continue until the full impact of the promotion could be determined. They argued that it might take several months before the promotional efforts had an impact on all customers. In particular, low users of long distance may have to be reminded several times about the offer before they remembered and had the opportunity to take advantage of the 5 free minutes. They also pointed out that the number of free minutes was highlighted on the customer's telephone bill and that this would help communicate the benefits of taking advantage of the discount. Many customers would have only received one or two telephone bills with the number of free long-distance minutes listed, so the full impact of the bills might not have been felt yet.

The discount continued, but it appeared to be losing money so in February senior management decided to end the trial. New advertisements were designed to inform the public that the discount would end April 30, 1985. In the first week of April, before the advertising was run, the marketing department conducted telephone interviews with adults in 401 households to measure people's awareness of the discount, their attitudes toward the discount, and how they felt the discount had affected their long-distance calling patterns.

The survey found that 97 percent of adults were aware of the discount and almost all understood how it worked. Seventy-four percent of the respondents said that, in their opinion, nobody in their household had changed their long-distance calling patterns because of the discount. The 26 percent that did feel there had been a change all indicated that they had talked longer. Many also indicated that they had switched from the daytime to the evening discount period or had called less often.

A tracking study of the household's long-distance usage was conducted in order to examine how those who had claimed to have taken advantage of the offer had changed their calling patterns. The tracking study recorded several facts about every call made by the 401 households covering a period of 3 months before the trial (June to August 1984), the 8 months during the discount offer (September 1984 to April 1985) and 3 months after the trial (May to July 1985). Included in the recorded facts was the length of the call in minutes, the cost of the call, the time of day, day of week and month. This amounted to over 500,000 pieces of data to be analyzed. The marketing manager had several objectives in analyzing the data. These included:

Objective 1 : to determine how the customers responded to the discount offer. Did they talk longer, call less often, and spend more or less per call? If they spent less per call, then management's theory on how the discount would affect revenue was wrong. However, if the trial discount generated calls, then this suggested the advertising should have stressed the fact that you couldn't take advantage of the special discount unless you called long distance. It might also suggest that the discount structure should be changed to stimulate more calls rather than longer ones, for example, a 3-minute discount after the first 5 minutes.

Objective 2 : to determine how these calling patterns changed over the trial period. Were there indications that the trial was more profitable as the trial progressed? It was noted that normally the length of long-distance calls increased until mid-winter and then declined to the low point in mid-summer. There was the basic question whether the discount would be more effective reinforcing or countering a trend. If it was the latter, then the discount should have been more profitable during the spring months (Jan–April). This would suggest that future discount offers be designed to counter trends in calling patterns that lead to reduced revenue.

Objective 3 : to determine how customers responded to the April advertisements announcing the end of the trial on April 30th. It was hypothesized that there would be a burst of long-distance calling in April as customers used their last chance to take advantage of the sale. If, however, there was a dramatic cutback in the number of calls, or the length of calls, this might suggest that customers misunderstood the ads and assumed the discount trial was already over.

Objective 4 : to examine the impact of the offer on Sunday and daytime calling patterns. The forecast department had decided to ignore these discount periods in their analysis of the offer's impact. This meant that there were no forecasts developed against which the marketing manager could measure the impact of the offer. He did know that the number of daytime calls and minutes was not supposed to vary more than 3 percent over the period of the trial which might be useful if the effects of the offer were substantially greater than 3 percent. However, Sunday was more of a problem since Christmas, the New Year, Mother's Day, and Easter all fell on Sundays during the trial. It was not known how much these holidays would affect calling patterns, but they certainly introduced a large amount of variability into the data making predictions of what the calling patterns might have been without the offer extremely difficult to judge.

The majority of the analysis would focus on those who had claimed to have taken advantage of the discount offer, but as a first step the marketing manager had the average long-distance minutes, calls, and revenue for each of the discount periods (business day, Sunday, evening, and night) for the 14 months calculated and printed by the company's mainframe computer. Once the averages were available, the manager entered them, and the forecast estimates, into the micro computer on his desk. With the aid of a spreadsheet program, he then produced several tables which, in general terms, indicated the effects of the discount on long-distance calling patterns.

The first step of his analysis was to adjust the monthly figures to reflect the number of days in the month (shorter months were increased proportionately) so that each month was comparable. He then converted the forecasts into indices so that they could be used with the sample data. This he did by dividing the average for the 3 months prior to the trial into the values for each of the 14 months. An index value of 1.15 meant that the month was forecast to be 15 percent higher than the average for the 3 months before the trial (the tables on your disk have already been adjusted for the days in the month and the forecasts converted to indices). These four tables are on your disk as a *Lotus* spreadsheet called **Arctic** and are printed in section 11.1.2.

He decided he needed a table which showed the deviations between the actual evening and nightime calls, minutes, and minutes-per-call, and the forecasts developed by the forecast department. While he could have done this in one step, he instead created a series of tables which illustrated the calling patterns that lead to the deviations derived on the last table. This allowed him to analyze the changes in consumer behavior, and having the tables would be useful for presenting his results to management. He also wanted to examine the calling patterns for Sunday and the business-day calling periods.

He next step was therefore to create a minutes-per-call table by dividing the monthly average minutes by the monthly average calls. His next table was a revenue-per-call table created in a similar fashion. Then he created five more tables which contained indices for calls, minutes, minutes per call, revenue per call, and revenue. The indices were created using the average for the 3 months prior to the trial as a base, the same as the forecast indices (see Table 5 on the spreadsheet as an example of how this is done). He then created the table that showed the differences between actual and forecast indices for calls, minutes and minutes per call (this table has the same format as Table 4 on the spreadsheet). He did not have forecasted figures for revenue, but could use the forecasted average minutes as an approximation of forecasted revenue since long distance is charged by the minute and the revenue per minute tended to be fairly constant throughout the year.

With these tables, he was able to do an initial analysis of the impact of the discount offer. The results of this initial analysis would be used as a guide to further analysis and preliminary recommendations for improved discount offers to follow.

11.1.1 Assignment

Create the tables and assume you are going to present your conclusions on how consumers responded to the offer and whether there is an opportunity for improving the discount offer to make it more profitable.

HINTS: Make extensive use of replicate or copy when deriving your tables. If the case is being presented, and time permits, then graphs can be created and used for the presentation (either directly off the screen or printed and turned into overheads).

11.1.2   Promotion Test Data

Table 1

Average Monthly Long Distance
Calls per Month

Months	Business Day	Sunday 8AM-6PM	Evening 6PM-10PM	Night 10PM-8AM	Total
June 84	3.27	0.39	1.92	0.99	6.56
July 84	3.25	0.36	1.64	0.78	6.03
August 84	3.49	0.33	1.71	0.92	6.45
Sept. 84	2.84	0.35	1.77	0.72	5.68
Oct. 84	2.83	0.39	2.03	0.83	6.07
Nov. 84	3.03	0.42	1.99	0.75	6.19
Dec. 84	3.32	0.58	2.00	0.87	6.78
Jan. 84	3.12	0.44	1.87	0.74	6.18
Feb. 85	2.96	0.44	1.86	0.71	5.97
March 85	3.51	0.45	2.01	0.77	6.74
April 85	3.14	0.48	1.89	0.75	6.27
May 85	3.22	0.40	2.01	0.96	6.59
June 85	3.32	0.38	1.92	1.00	6.62
July 85	3.47	0.39	1.94	0.92	6.73

Table 2

Average Monthly Long Distance
Minutes per Household

Months	Business Day	Sunday 8AM-6PM	Evening 6PM-10PM	Night 10PM-8AM	Total
June 84	12.51	2.05	10.97	5.45	30.98
July 84	12.40	1.67	8.72	5.13	27.92
August 84	13.57	1.47	9.71	5.12	29.87
Sept. 84	11.54	1.73	12.03	4.52	29.82
Oct. 84	11.21	2.26	13.17	5.55	32.19
Nov. 84	13.10	2.32	13.19	5.11	33.71
Dec. 84	13.58	3.83	13.57	5.78	36.76
Jan. 85	13.34	2.73	13.56	5.06	34.69
Feb. 85	11.98	2.26	13.60	5.06	32.90
March 85	15.64	2.22	14.29	5.49	37.64
April 85	13.03	2.40	13.08	4.40	32.91
May 85	12.76	2.33	13.37	6.75	35.20
June 85	12.67	1.88	12.36	6.19	33.10
July 85	13.48	1.74	10.64	5.54	31.40

Table 3

Average Monthly Long Distance
Revenue per Household

Months	Business Day	Sunday 8AM-6PM	Evening 6PM-10PM	Night 10PM-8AM	Total
June 84	$4.11	$0.48	$2.68	$1.18	$8.45
July 84	$4.12	$0.40	$2.14	$1.12	$7.78
August 84	$4.37	$0.33	$2.48	$1.13	$8.31
Sept. 84	$3.57	$0.40	$2.59	$0.87	$7.44
Oct. 84	$3.44	$0.57	$2.86	$1.00	$7.87
Nov. 84	$3.91	$0.57	$2.82	$1.00	$8.30
Dec. 84	$4.14	$0.95	$3.00	$1.09	$9.18
Jan. 85	$4.09	$0.65	$2.92	$1.03	$8.68
Feb. 85	$3.83	$0.55	$2.94	$1.02	$8.34
March 85	$5.07	$0.59	$3.19	$1.07	$9.92
April 85	$4.23	$0.67	$2.76	$0.87	$8.53
May 85	$4.10	$0.61	$3.21	$1.53	$9.46
June 85	$4.03	$0.52	$2.88	$1.35	$8.78
July 85	$4.04	$0.38	$2.47	$1.15	$8.04

Table 4

Forecasted Percent Deviation from
June to August Averages:
Calls, Minutes and Minutes-per-Call

	Calls		Minutes		Minutes/Call	
Months	Evening	Night	Evening	Night	Evening	Night
Sept. 84	4.98%	-10.27%	9.96%	-9.86%	4.36%	0.46%
Oct. 84	2.07%	-13.23%	6.52%	-10.34%	4.35%	3.33%
Nov. 84	-0.54%	-13.17%	10.95%	-7.78%	11.55%	6.20%
Dec. 84	-1.45%	-4.53%	9.92%	1.39%	11.55%	6.20%
Jan. 85	-8.13%	-17.10%	7.44%	-7.20%	16.95%	11.94%
Feb. 85	-7.82%	-16.48%	9.46%	-8.90%	18.76%	9.07%
March 85	1.25%	-6.37%	14.78%	-0.56%	13.37%	6.20%
April 85	1.05%	-8.63%	10.91%	-2.96%	9.75%	6.20%
May 85	5.24%	0.05%	11.71%	4.82%	6.15%	4.77%
June 85	5.72%	12.05%	8.42%	15.77%	2.55%	3.33%
July 85	3.69%	11.80%	0.74%	9.10%	-2.85%	-2.41%

Table 5

Indexed Average Monthly Household Calls Per Month

Months	Business Day	Sunday 8AM-6PM	Evening 6PM-10PM	Night 10PM-8AM	Total
June 84	-1.96%	7.93%	9.17%	10.24%	3.41%
July 84	-2.65%	0.00%	-6.55%	-12.65%	-4.99%
August 84	4.61%	-7.93%	-2.62%	2.41%	1.59%
Sept. 84	-14.80%	-3.06%	0.90%	-19.59%	-10.46%
Oct. 84	-15.18%	7.49%	15.53%	-7.75%	-4.34%
Nov. 84	-9.00%	17.09%	12.85%	-15.84%	-2.43%
Dec. 84	-0.28%	62.00%	13.87%	-2.92%	6.80%
Jan. 85	-6.33%	23.80%	6.47%	-16.94%	-2.57%
Feb. 85	-11.08%	22.13%	5.58%	-20.32%	-5.88%
March 85	5.44%	24.50%	14.02%	-13.67%	6.20%
April 85	-5.74%	34.30%	7.56%	-15.82%	-1.21%
May 85	-3.42%	12.67%	14.17%	7.07%	3.85%
June 85	-0.27%	5.85%	8.91%	11.87%	4.33%
July 85	4.20%	7.52%	10.56%	3.04%	5.99%

11.2   Creating Tables and Graphs

Most of you will have had some experience with spreadsheet packages. However, we are often rusty and would appreciate some guidance to get us back into it easily. To this end, we have included some step-by-step instructions for creating a table and a graph on *Lotus*. For the table, at least, the commands will be similar to those for other spreadsheet programs.

11.2.1   Creating a Table

Copying the Headings

First, copy a table that has the same format and headings as the table you wish to create.

1. Move the cursor to cell A112.

2. Type the command key "/".

3. Use the arrow keys to highlight the Copy command; hit return.

4. A range of A112..A112 is already specified. Use the arrow keys to change the second cell reference to F131. Hit return.

5. The program will now ask you to enter the range to which to copy. **Important**: do not simply hit return at this point or you may erase the whole area you highlighted to copy. Use the arrow keys to specify A140 as the destination for the copy and then hit return.

6. The cursor will return to cell A112. Use the arrow keys to move to A140 and see what you have copied.

Entering the Title

1. Move to cell C134 and type *Table 6*.

2. Move to cell B136 and type *Average Minutes per Call*. (Don't worry if there are more letters than usually fit in a cell; the program looks after that.)

Creating the Data

1. Move to cell B143. You will create a new formula in the cell so that the desired value is displayed.

2. Start the formula by typing a left parenthesis "(".

3. The formula is (average June Business Day Minutes/average June Business Day Calls). Use the PgUp key to move to Table 2. The average June Business Day Minutes are stored in cell B38. Highlight this cell and hit return to enter the cell reference into your formula.

4. Type the command key "/".

5. Use the Home key to move up to Table 1 and highlight the average June Business Day Calls per month in cell B13 and hit return to enter this cell reference into your formula.

6. Type in the right bracket ")" to finish the formula and hit return to enter the formula into the cell.

Changing the Format

The old table had a percent format. You will want to change the format to a fixed format with two decimal places.

1. Hit the command key "/".

2. Use the arrow key to highlight the Range command and hit return.

3. Hit return again to format the cell.

4. Select the fixed format by hitting return.

5. Select two decimal places by hitting return.

6. For range, you could specify the whole table, but you will be copying the cell anyway so this is not necessary. Just hit return to specify the cell B143.

Copying the Cell

1. Hit the command key "/".

2. Type *C* (a small *c* will work just as well) to go to the Copy command.

3. A "From" range of B143..B143 will already be specified. Simply hit return. If you make a mistake anywhere along the way, try hitting the escape key ESC to go back a step or two and make corrections.

4. The "To" range will start with B143. Hit the period key to specify the B143 as the first range value.

5. Use the arrow keys to specify F156 as the second range value; hit return.

Fixing the Average Line

1. Move to cell B158.

2. Hit the edit key F2, one of the function keys on the left of the keyboard.

3. Use the left arrow to move the cursor under the 4 in B44.

4. Type in *143*, and hit the delete button twice to change B44 to B143. Repeat the process to change the other two cell references to B144 and B145. Hit return to enter the new formula.

5. Change the format to fixed with two decimal places and copy the cell to the range B158..F158.

   Congratulations, you have now created Table 6.

11.2.2 Creating a Graph

Assume you wish to create a graph showing the indexed calls per month using the data in Table 5.

1. Move to cell B118. You will be graphing the September 84 to July 85 data in cells B118 to B128.

2. Hit the command key "/", then type *G* for the Graph command.

3. Type *T* to specify type of graph and then *L* to specify a line graph. Then hit return.

4. Next specify the labels for the X axis. Type *X* and move the cursor to G118. We have included a column of letters representing the first letter of the month for you to use as labels. Normally you might use the labels in cells A118 to A128 but they do not fit along the bottom

of the graph. Hit the period key to designate that cell as the range start, then use the arrow keys to highlight the remaining cells down to G128 and then hit return.

5. Type A to specify the first range of values to be graphed. Highlight B118 and then hit the period key to specify the start of the range. Use the arrow key to move down to B128 and hit return.

6. Repeat step 5 for B, C, and D using the cell ranges C118..C128, D118..D128, and E118..E128 respectively.

7. Type O for options. Hit return to enter the legend values. Hit return to enter the legend for value set A. Type in *Business Day* or some other suitable legend to name the first set of values. Repeat the process for value sets B, C, and D.

8. While still in the options menu, type T for titles and type in an appropriate title.

9. Type Q to quit this menu.

10. Type V to view your graph. Hit any key to stop viewing the graph.

11. Type N to name the graph, then type C to save the graph you have created and give it a name. When you save the spreadsheet data, the graph specifications will also be saved.

12. Type Q to quit the graph menu.

13. You will be able to call up this graph by:

    (a) Hitting, command key "/".

    (b) Typing G for the Graph command.

    (c) Type N for name.

    (d) Hitting return to make a named graph the current graph.

    (e) Highlight the graph you want to display and hit return. This displays the graph and sets all the graph values (type, X, B, C, etc.) to those of the displayed graph.

14. If you have created a series of graphs, you can simulate a slide show by hitting return which puts you into Name, hitting return again which puts you into Use, hitting return again to bring up the list of graphs, highlighting the desired graph and hitting return again. Three quick returns, a graph selection, and another return will show your next graph. Repeat these steps to show all your graphs. It isn't great, but in a pinch it is better than nothing.